WELCOME
TO THE
SPIRIT WORLD

An Explanation of Metaphysics

Sharon Margolis

authorHOUSE®

AuthorHouse™
1663 Liberty Drive
Bloomington, IN 47403
www.authorhouse.com
Phone: 1 (800) 839-8640

Published by AuthorHouse 07/26/2018

ISBN: 978-1-5462-5165-1 (sc)
ISBN: 978-1-5462-5164-4 (e)

Library of Congress Control Number: 2018908328

Print information available on the last page.

TO RUTH

My white wolf

CONTENTS

INTRODUCTION

Welcome to the spirit world.

Allow me to introduce you to the universe of metaphysics. Based on my personal experiences, these chapters explain the fundamental concepts of psychic phenomena. Take my hand and let us begin our voyage…

We journeyed to the land of the dead, danced in the eternal light, delved into spirit worlds none of us dreamed existed. Specters of the dark side guided us through their realms: Shaman in the twilight wolf wilderness, Spirit Bird in the Valley Of The Birds, Joel the medieval Irishman in the record of all time.

While on the other side my thoughts and emotions were shared first by my friend Ruth, and later by others as though we had one mind. I felt their fears and desires, their awe and adventurous spirit. They knew mine as well. Yet back in our body we could only communicate through the spoken word.

The fact that other people see the same visions as I while traveling in the spirit world is verification to me that my view of the outer regions is not just the product of my colorful imagination. The spirit world truly exists.

Ruth and I thought our travels together were wondrous accidents until it happened again and again. Each experience was more complex and powerful than the last. Our journeys were never planned, nor did we discuss beforehand places we had discovered while there alone. Neither of us wanted to plant subconscious hints as to where we should go or what we should do. But once we were there, we led each other to our secret places, dimensions and past lives that the other person did not know existed.

Considering Ruth's and my own diverse backgrounds, the fact that our journeys were so similar is especially striking. Ruth was born to Christian parents in a small town in Wisconsin. She was taught in the ways of the church, and was spiritually born again. Her psychic abilities came to her as a child, when she left her body during a time of stress, and travelled to the wolf place. The wolf wilderness became her special sanctuary when she felt troubled. At the age of nineteen Ruth moved to Southern California. There she learned the rudiments of metaphysics from her sister who was also Christian. Ruth's religious affiliations have always been with a strong Christian base.

I was raised in an Orthodox Jewish family in Brooklyn New York, and married within that religion. My first lessons in the occult came through the books of Tuesday Lobsang Rampa. He was a Tibetan Lama whose teachings were popular in the 1970's. At that time I also discovered yoga, both hatha (physical positions) and meditation. Yoga was my introduction to meditation. The meditation included relaxation, breathing exercises, and occasionally a guided meditation where the teacher told the class what to see, hear and feel. I did not think of the guided meditations as astral travel journeys. My beginner series of yoga sessions was part of a community extension course, and was held at night in a high school gymnasium. The mundane surroundings, and the way the teacher conducted the class did not appease my curiosity about metaphysics. Mind-teasing subjects like channeling, angel guides, and astral travel were not mentioned.

A few months after the beginner yoga classes ended I moved to California. That was in January of 1973. I soon found an intermediate yoga class. It was primarily hatha yoga with a meditation at the end of each session. Alice, my instructor, did not teach metaphysics, but she acknowledged its existence. One evening during a class meditation, I felt my consciousness float in the air. One minute my eyes were closed, and I felt my yoga mat that I was lying on touching my body from the back of my head down to my heels. The next minute I could no longer feel my body. It was night and only one candle flickered in the room so no light seeped through my shut eyelids. All was dark.

And then the beast appeared.

It was a darker form in the dark surrounding me. The only distinct shapes were its huge eyes. Even though I knew my body was safe on the material plane, I was terrified. I did not know what to expect, and the absence of light around the beast concerned me. To me light means a positive force. Then I saw sorrow in those eyes. There was something familiar in the creature's expression. After a minute of trying to understand who it reminded me of I got the impression it was my sister Barbara who lived in New York. She had deep-seated emotion problems, and had just come out of a mental hospital. My fear dissipated, but I still felt uneasy. If this was what Barbara looked like inside her soul, she was in a lot of pain. I sent out mind messages to make contact with her to comfort her, but she was unresponsive.

Anxiety rushed through me that my teacher was going to call us out of meditation with her usual tonal "ohm". I pushed that feeling aside with the determination to reach my sister before I went back to the earth plane. The dark spirit's huge paw extended toward me. I reached my hand toward it, and at the moment of contact the paw turned into the long-fingered, artistic human hand of Barbara. An instant later I heard Alice toning me back to wakefulness.

The flight out of the void took only a few seconds. Again my yoga mat felt scratchy against my bare heels, and the hard floor beneath the mat was firm against my shoulders and head. I was back. Shaken, but back.

My teacher came to me as I sat up. "Are you alright, Sharon?" she asked, concern in her voice. "What happened? I wanted to call everyone back, but I heard you in my head telling me, 'No. Not yet!' You sounded upset so I waited."

I told Alice about my vision, and she seemed mystified. She had no experience with that sort of thing, and could not explain it or help me. I was so upset with the unsettling insight into Barbara, and my lack of control and understanding of what had happened, and could happen to me in that level of meditation that I avoided it for the next five years.

Taking into account my leanings toward the oriental philosophies, it was natural that I converted to Buddhism. In 1979 I officially changed my religion to the Japanese Nicheren sect of Buddhism. One day shortly after my conversion I was chanting during my daily practice, and felt myself flying up. My eyes were closed, but I saw clouds floating below me. The physicality of chanting on the dense material plane kept me grounded enough that I felt comfortable, and more in control than during my first out-of-body experience. For years I only astral traveled while chanting.

Ruth and I met while teaching Project Self-Esteem at the elementary school our children attended. After speaking about our spiritual beliefs we realized that we thought alike on many issues. We called the concepts we shared by different names, but there was little if any difference in the meaning. We have deep respect for each other's belief system.

In 1995, a few days after my mother died, her spirit channeled through my body. For me that was a time of emotional upheaval, and also the beginning of great spiritual growth. Ruth, recognizing my need for a pacifying influence, suggested we meditate together.

And so our journeys began.

At the start we were curious, but tentative about what was happening to us. We only went to places on the astral planes that one or the other of us knew. There was reassurance in the familiar. I followed Ruth to her wolf wilderness, and she came with me to the Akashic Record to view some of my past lives. Our capabilities expanded with time and practice.

During the next few years we journeyed together off and on. I attended classes in astral travel and channeling at The Learning Light Foundation, and we made use of my newfound abilities to deepen and expand our experiences. I met my guide Joel, Ruth had Shaman, and the four of us traveled together.

This book tells of my experiences on the astral planes with Ruth, alone and with other travelers. It also includes explanations of metaphysical topics such as astral travel, channeling, and metaphysical energy. This should help you to understand the goings on during my journeys, as well as afford you a sound base for further investigations. The information given in these chapters barely scratches the surface of each subject. I urge you to seek more deeply into any topic that piques your interest.

CHAPTER ONE

CHILDREN IN THE LIGHT

JOURNAL ENTRY
NOVEMBER 1

The two of us sat on pillows facing each other on the floor of Ruth's wolf room. Dim light flickered from a single pillar candle on a nearby table, illuminating pictures and statues of wolves and Native American artifacts, covering every surface. Sweet floral incense wafted on the early evening air.

This was our first time meditating together. Neither of us knew what to expect. We reached out and lightly held hands.

I closed my eyes, relaxed, breathed in, and called the light (the universal energy) to enter me. It would not come. Blackness came in its place, holding me back from the light. Undisturbed, I decided to focus on seeing Ruth's aura. I saw her light, but it was dormant, not much movement or heat. Her energy was closed off, pulling inward. At my mental call the eternal force flowed from my fingers to her hands. It circled through our physical and astral bodies, enveloping us in radiance.

My soul called to hers, "Come with me, Ruth. Come with me into the light."

I saw her energy unfurl like a flower, gaining in volume and brilliance. I felt the light filling me as well as we ascended to the sky. We were surrounded in blue sky with puffy white clouds in the distance. Sunlight poured over us while we whirled round and round, dancing, holding our faces up to the heat source. My mind's eye saw us as children, our long golden hair twirling around us as we laughed.

"Dance with me, Ruth, dance," my spirit voice sang out.

I savored the glorious feeling, drinking in the energy. The energy started to drain from me and the image faded away. Earth was calling me back.

I hummed, giving the signal we had agreed upon to return to this world. Our eyes opened to the candlelit wolf room. We were quiet for a short while, both of us unsure of how to begin.

I do not remember who spoke first, but Ruth recalled the oppressive darkness she saw at the beginning. She had also asked the light to enter us both, felt its warm energy flow back and forth between us, saw it course through our body. She too spoke of us dancing in the sunlight, holding hands, rejuvenating until we were children, her feeling of elation. As we spoke the similarity of our experiences became obvious.

I was doubly astonished. For twenty-five years I had meditated, but never thought what I did was astral travel. The usual accounts of a person's soul rising above its body and seeing it from above was not in my experience. Yet, Ruth who goes out-of-body in that way met me outside. Even more astounding, we communicated there, not with words, but by feeling the other person's emotions. Both of us felt the other's joy. I was using psychic abilities I thought I did not have. All of my meditations through the years when I had the same awareness as in that experience with Ruth of being in a "different" place took on a new meaning for me. I had been in the astral then too. My concept of my metaphysical talents and my place in the universe suddenly changed. Many metaphysical phenomena I had read about were suddenly possible future experiences for me. My curiosity took wing.

ASTRAL TRAVEL

The spirit world, also known as the higher astral planes, is all around us. We cannot see it, hear it, smell it or touch it, but it is here. Our physical perceptions are limited. Germs are too minute for us to see with the naked eye and odors are invisible particles in the air of whatever it is we smell.

Animals can pick up scents and hear sound frequencies, which a human cannot. Obviously, the dependability of our sensory organs is lacking.

Energy on the higher astral planes vibrates at a higher frequency than we can detect with our physical body. In order to make the leap between this plane, called the physical plane or material plane, and the higher astral planes, we must raise the frequency of our personal energy field.

Each person has an energy field. It is called an aura. Depending on our personality, emotional and physical wellbeing, our aura will take on different colors. Colors in general are determined by energy vibrations (frequencies), infrared being the slowest and ultra-violet the fastest. Some people can see auras. They are capable of seeing that frequency of light. My friend Eleanor was born with that capability to such an extent that it has always been a normal part of her life. One day in a classroom there was a student sitting in front of her whose aura was so high and bright Eleanor had to move to another seat to see the blackboard.

She taught me to see auras. If the person whose aura I am trying to see stands in front of a single-colored background, I can look around the head, not at it, and see waves emanating from the head like seeing heat floating up from a black top road on a hot day. Then the light shines out and takes form. My talent at reading auras is very minimal. I do not see colors, only a mixed gold and white light, and cannot get meaning from what I see. When I am channeling with my eyes closed I still see only a gold and white light, but I can read about the person from his energy field.

So, we all have an energy field called an aura. If we raise the frequency of this aura high enough, we can reach the vibration of the higher astral planes. While I did it spontaneously during meditation or chanting for my Buddhist practice, that method was inconsistent at best. I never intentionally chanted to astral travel. It just happened. How or why is still a mystery to me. When astral traveling with Ruth the first few times I just relaxed, and imagined myself flying up. That worked, but I felt lost up there, unfocused and unsure of what to do. Since then I have been taught many methods of rising out of my body and starting on a journey. The method I usually use, which I describe in this chapter, affords me a degree of control and feeling of safety with which I am comfortable.

Basically, all meditation is a form of self-hypnosis. The first steps to all the methods of astral travel are the same as being put into a hypnotic state. Although I explain the process in easy detailed steps, I do not expect the reader to use them to astral travel. In my experience, we learn best by doing. Get someone who knows how to teach you in person.

STEP 1. SIT OR LIE DOWN IN A COMFORTABLE POSITION.

STEP 2. BREATHE IN SLOWLY AND DEEPLY. BREATHE OUT SLOWLY AND COMPLETELY. REPEAT THREE TIMES. Continue to breathe slowly and deeply throughout the journey,

STEP 3. RELAX EACH PART OF YOUR BODY. Start at the top of your head and slowly work down your face, head, neck, shoulders, arms, etc. until your entire body is relaxed.

STEP 4. IMAGINE YOURSELF SLOWLY TAKING SIX STEPS DOWN A STAIRWAY. WITH EACH STEP GO DEEPER INTO RELAXATION. This last step I learned at a hypnosis certification seminar. The technique also came up in a few astral travel classes I attended. One teacher told us to step inside a hollow tree and down into the earth. The other had us entering a cave and going down. Both shamanic methods were done as STEP 5 after the energy work. I do the energy work as STEP 5.

As we can see, the first four steps help us to relax. The next steps deal with raising our frequency of vibrations. The steps past four are metaphysical in nature and were not taught to me in hypnosis classes. There are energy points on the spine called chakras. For now I will give a brief explanation. In a future chapter I will devote more time to it.

The most accepted number of charkas is seven. Other belief systems say there are more. Each chakra gives off energy at a different frequency and is seen as a different color. Starting at the base of the spine and going up to the top of the head, the colors are: first, red for the root, which is the lowest frequency, second is orange at the genitals, third is yellow in the stomach area, fourth is green for the heart, fifth is above that with blue at the throat, sixth is violet between the eyebrows, topped by the crown chakra on top of the head which is white. I see the crown chakra as white light with gold sparkles interspersed. Energy frequencies are higher as the chakra is higher on the body. The bottom three charkas ground us. We use the top four to help leave the earth plane.

STEP 5. IMAGINE A GREEN SWIRL SLOWLY EMINATING FROM THE HEART CHAKRA, GROWING AND PULSING AROUND YOU WITH EACH HEARTBEAT. Feel its energy flowing through your body. Now see a blue light flowing from the throat chakra, growing and dancing with the green. From the third eye chakra, purple energy floats out and mixes with the swirling green and blue. Feel the combined heat of the energies glowing in your body, rising to the top of your head. Open the crown chakra, the white point on the top of your head. See its light combine with the green, blue and purple, swirling all around you.

STEP 6. IMAGINE THE WHITE AND GOLD LIGHT OF THE CROWN CHAKRA SHAPING ITSELF INTO A COLUMN, RISING INTO THE SKY. See yourself flying up into that column of light, ascending into the sky, through the clouds and above. Feel the air rushing past your face, the tingle of energy through your astral body as you fly up. The sky is blue all around you with cottony clouds below. A freestanding portal (open doorway) appears and you stand before it. Some people call it a vortex. The doorway is only a symbol of the change in energy frequency that allows us onto the higher astral planes. Not everyone sees it as a door. I use it as a tool to cross over to the spirit world.

STEP 7. COVER YOURSELF WITH THE WHITE LIGHT FOR PROTECTION AGAINST NEGATIVE FORCES OR BEINGS. See yourself in the center of a bubble of white light. Say a short prayer for protection. The one printed below is only a suggestion.

I AM SURROUNDED IN THE WHITE LIGHT, LOVE AND PROTECTION OF POSITIVE FORCES (GOD) NOW AND ALWAYS. ASSIST ME WITH BRINGING IN THE HIGHEST TEACHERS I CAN HANDLE AT THIS TIME. IN THE LIGHT OF PROTECTION I ASK FOR MESSAGES OF TRUTH AND LOVE.
GUIDES, BE WITH ME NOW!

We ask for protection because there are entities that can harm us when we leave our body. I rarely encounter evil in the spirit world, but when I do the guide or totem I am traveling with always protects me. I try not to astral travel without a guide.

STEP 8. CONTACT YOUR GUIDE. Look through the portal. You still stand above the clouds in daylight, but you see the night sky and stars on the other side of the open doorway. See a light float toward you. It grows larger and more brilliant as it draws near. The light floats through the doorway, and takes form.

There are different kinds of guides: animals, angels, spirits of those you know who have passed on, ascended masters, many kinds of spirits or beings who have or have not lived on this world. A future chapter will cover the subject of guides more in depth. I always travel with a guide not only for protection, but because they are wonderful sources of information and clarification. Astral travel communicates to us like a dreamscape. In fact, we all can astral travel while we sleep and often do. The things we see, hear, and feel while in the spirit world are symbols, and vary from person to person. We relate to our universe in different ways. Some of us are clairvoyant, meaning we see pictures. Others are clairaudient, hearing sounds or words. There are also sensitives who feel or experience a "knowing". Another form of experiencing information is through empathy, feeling the emotions of others. I use all these methods, but am more of an empath than anything else. I also see and read energy. When we have trouble interpreting a symbol we can ask our guide for clarification.

A few years ago Nila who is a practitioner of Wicca went out of body with me. We wound up in ancient Egypt. Curious how she knew she was in Egypt, I asked her what she saw that led her to that conclusion. She said her symbol for Egypt was the pyramids. That was what she saw. I saw the Egyptian god Horus with the body of a man and the head of a falcon. Horus is my symbol for Egypt. We saw different things, but both knew we were in the same place.

Ask your guide's name so you can call it to you again on another journey. If you do not receive a name from the guide, give it a name.

STEP 9. SET AN INTENTION. What is your purpose for contacting the spirit plane this particular time? Is there someone who has passed away who you would like to contact, a question about your past, present or future you would like answered or about someone else? Do you have a problem you need help in solving? Your purpose does not need to be specific. In fact, you do not need a purpose at all. You can ask your guide to give you messages that would benefit you at that time. If you travel without a purpose, the symbols you see are more likely to need interpretation by your guide. Do not hesitate to ask questions for clarification. Tell your guide your intention for the journey.

STEP 10. GO THROUGH THE DOORWAY. Fly with your guide into the night sky on the other side of the doorway. You feel the sensation of flying in outer space. Do not try to project your destination into your thoughts. Allow your guide to take you where it will.

Astral Travel is much like aware dreams. There are frequent unexpected scene changes with characters moving in and out in a nonsensical jumble. The pictures, sounds, and smells are not material things, only methods of communication between us and our guide or with whatever entity we make contact. Sometimes we do not knowingly travel with a guide, but I believe there is always one with us.

We each have three bodies in this material life. One is the physical body that we are familiar with, the one that experiences through its senses, and we dress in clothing. The other two are etheric bodies that consist of energy. Our etheric bodies are the ones that astral travel while the physical body remains on the physical plane. There is a cord made of silver light that connects the etheric bodies to the navel of the physical body. When one etheric body travels to the astral planes we call it astral travel. When two etheric bodies leave the physical body, and they are tethered by the silver cord we call it astral projection. That is the near death experience we hear about when we float above our body, and see ourself, and what is happening below, but cannot move or communicate with anyone. When two etheric bodies leave the physical body, and the silver cord is broken, we call it death. All of us astral travel when we sleep. Some of us experience astral projection during that time. The two etheric bodies are shaped like the physical body. They travel as one form with two layers.

During meditation I only astral travel. I have never felt the need to try astral projection. While it is true that remote viewing (seeing the physical world from the astral planes) is easier during astral projection, I can travel freely on the astral planes, visit the Akashic Record, communicate with guides, shape-shift into animal form, speak with departed souls, and do many other wonderful things while only astral traveling.

STEP 11. RETURN TO THE PHYSICAL PLANE. When you have achieved your intention, you find it difficult to hold your concentration or your physical body feels uncomfortable it is time to return to the earth plane. Ask your guide to take you back to the doorway. When you arrive there, thank your guide for its help and release it. Step through the doorway. Shut down the chakras, starting with the crown. See the gold-white light go out. Shut down the violet third eye, then the blue light at the throat, last the green heart chakra. Imagine all the extra energy that fills your body is seeping down toward your feet, and out into the ground like the roots of a tree until your body is empty of it. Count backwards from six, moving toward wakefulness with each count. If you do not ground yourself, you will feel spaced-out.

I hope this explanation of astral travel has given you a base of understanding upon which the following chapters can build. There is also a glossary at the back of this book.

CHAPTER TWO

WOLF IN THE WILDERNESS

JOURNAL ENTRY
NOVEMBER 8

I joined Ruth in the sky, floating lazily among the clouds, tranquil and content. Suddenly, she flew up and away at a zooming speed.

"Wait for me! Slow down!" I called in mind-speak, starting after her.

Ruth reached back, grabbed my outstretched hand, and together we raced among the stars. We alighted in a dark wilderness. Dense fog swirled around us. Stark silhouettes of denuded trees reminded me of a forest in winter. Cold dampness filled my lungs, a strange sensation indeed since on the less dense astral plane I had no physical body.

In the shadows of the twilight dimness I made out the slinking forms of wolves. While apprehension, curiosity, and excitement kept my nerves strung tight, I felt no fear. This place was strange, but instinct told me Ruth was comfortable here, and would protect me.

To my amazement, Ruth changed into a wolf. Her fur was white, and she was almost invisible in the fog. I picked up from her mental messages that she wanted me to join her in animal form, but that seemed too alien to me. I stood back, and watched her run and howl with the other wolves. She soon returned to me, and resumed her human appearance.

We hugged on the astral plane, knowing it was time to come back to earth.

Once Ruth and I were grounded, our astral bodies securely in the physical, we spoke of our journey. I use the singular for we were out there together, experiencing the same sensations. We communicated by feeling each other's emotions. The wilderness place was new to me. Ruth had never spoken of it in my presence, nor had she told me of her shape-shifting, I had not known of the wolf world before our journey.

We sat on the floor of the candlelit room. My spirit felt confined in my body. I tentatively spoke of being in the wilderness, and seeing the wolves. The astral experience was so bizarre that I did not expect Ruth to have had a similar one.

After I finished speaking, the room was quiet for a short while. Finally, she said, "You saw it. You saw my wolf. Why didn't you become one also? I wanted you to experience it."

Conceptually, I know what totems are, but had no experience with them before this, and they are not a part of my belief system. I have no idea why I said, "It's not my totem," as though I had ever given it a thought. When Ruth asked what my totem was I had no answer for her. Most of the next day I pondered, and meditated on the subject. A cougar came to mind, but there was some doubt, and I thought a discussion with Ruth might clear it up. Phoning her, I mentioned the cougar and she said, "Right form, wrong color. Your totem is the black panther."

She explained to me that since her childhood she has retreated to her secret wilderness place in her mind where it is always dusk, always winter, and she is accompanied by the white wolf and the black panther. After forty-five years she has found the wolf's companion. Ruth felt that me experiencing her wilderness world was like having me walk in her soul.

TOTEMS

Many ancient cultures all over the world practiced Shamanism. Some still do. Shamanic practitioners feel close to the land, communing with all parts of nature, including animals. Animals that we feel a soul relationship with are called totems. I do not mean our pets. The soul relationship meant here is our sharing common behaviors and energies with a species of animal or having a certain animal teach us a life lesson we currently need.

Every creature displays some characteristic of the power of the eternal light. For instance, one of my totem animals is beaver. My first reaction when beaver appeared to me was; no, that couldn't be right. It's a rodent! It's not pretty or sexy. It's not even cute. Then I considered its qualities. Beaver is always working, creating, building. Work, activity, and creativity are compulsions for me. I am happiest when accomplishing something, not necessarily finishing a task, but while doing it. Beaver has given me a deeper understanding of myself.

My formal introduction to Shamanism was through a four-hour class at The Learning Light Foundation. The Three Worlds were explained to us; upper world where human spirits reside, middle world which is the physical plane of earth, the awake world we know, and the lower world which is the place of animal spirits. The lower world is not filled with spirits of millions of animals. A wolf is not a totem. The collective essence or universal spirit of wolf or bear or deer is a totem. That is why I wrote, "one of my totem animals is beaver". Not a beaver, but the essence of beaver.

At the class, shamanic journeying was new to me in some ways, and familiar in other ways. I had been astral traveling with Ruth almost weekly for a couple of months, and wanted to learn about what I was already doing. Traveling in the form of an animal, also called shape-shifting, was something with which I was experienced. The traditions were all new to me.

We were a small class, only about seven or eight female students. First we were saged. The teacher, who was a young Native American woman, lit fire to a small wand of dried sage, letting the flame die down until it only smoked. The pungent scent of the burning herb tickled the inside of my nose. She waved it around each woman to cleanse her aura. This is a common practice at many spiritual and metaphysical gatherings. Sometimes people will sage a room to drive out negative energy.

We then all lay flat on our back on mats, and the teacher turned on a drumming tape. Shamanic journeying is traditionally done with a rapid, steady rhythm in the background, played on a handheld ceremonial drum. The teacher chose to play a recorded tape instead of drumming for us herself. I was led to the lower world by the teacher's monotone instructions. She did the deep breathing and muscle relaxing sequence.

Next we followed her into a hollow dead tree, and descended into the lower world. She set us free to wander, and meet what animals we would.

Black Panther came to me. It was a spirit animal I knew well from my travels with Ruth. Panther helped me to feel comfortable in the new environment. We traveled near each other. My spirit flew above the big cat and slightly behind, following as it led me into a forest. The ground below became a stream with a network of twig dams, creating a slow-moving waterway. I saw Beaver, and was introduced to my second totem. The drumming in the background seemed to pick up speed with the frenetic energy of Beaver. Panther and I soon left the forest behind, and I found myself in a sun-flooded meadow. Horse was running, his hooves pounding on the flower-covered field, mane flying behind him. Suddenly, I was Horse. The magnificent power in my muscles bunched and stretched as I sped in glorious freedom. Being a city girl I had never ridden a horse or had much to do with horses in general so this experience was a revelation to me. I have since heard that the meaning of the spirit of Horse is strength and freedom. Then the instructor called us back to the middle world. After thanking Horse, Beaver and Panther I returned to Earth. That shamanic journey seminar helped me to see the boundary of what I do naturally, and what is in the shamanic tradition. When I astral travel by myself I rarely see animals or become them. Only when I traveled with Ruth or am part of a shamanic group do I shape-shift.

Since that first seminar I have had many Shamanic group experiences. One of the things that stands out for me most is the similarities of what I call "the opening of the circle ceremony" in so many different cultures. It is how a pagan or shamanic leader convenes a group spiritual session by calling in spirits. The first time I saw the ceremony it was performed by a Wiccan. Wicca is the pagan religion of witches. Barbara, the speaker, was explaining Wicca during a metaphysical seminar. She started by standing and facing the East, calling in the powers (spirits) of that direction. She spoke in rhymes, lifting her arms in supplication. In turn she faced the other three directions, calling in the spirits of each. That seminar was many years ago, and I do not remember the details of it.

The second time I experienced it was at a drum circle held at a Native American shop called Four Crows. Daryl, the owner of the shop, is a Sundance Dancer, Pipe Carrier, and Ghost Dancer out of the Pine Ridge reservation. The drum circle at Four Crows was a meeting of people who played hand drums. At the start of each session Daryl entered the circle of drummers with his smoking sage pot, and "cleansed" each person by wafting smoke in his or her direction with an eagle feather while he spoke in the Lakota language. Then he called in the spirits of the six directions, east, south, west, north, sky above, and earth below. For this he faced each direction as he shook a long-handled rattle and intoned in Lakota. As I write this I recall the dim smoky light, the scent of burning sage, and Daryl's deep voice calling in the spirits.

For six years I went to monthly drum circles held at a metaphysical shop called Visions and Dreams that was vastly different from the one at Four Crows. Their drum circle was for people who astral traveled. At Visions and Dreams the drumming was done by the leader while everyone else traveled out-of-body. For the first few years Gretchen was our leader. In her opening the circle ceremony everyone in the group stood up, and rattled in the directions. As we faced each direction and rattled, she called in the animal spirits. It went something like this:

"Great spirits of the East we honor you, Be with us today Great Eagle, Swan and Hawk.

We call to you spirits of the South, Tiger and Coyote, Bring us your power.

Spirits of the West come to us, oh, Whale, Dolphin and beings of the sea.

Great ones of the North, Buffalo, Bear and Elk bring your wisdom into our circle.

Great spirits from above, heavenly ancestors, be with us now.

Nature spirits that dwell below help us today.

Spirit within, be open to messages for your highest good."

We then put down our rattles, and picked up our hand drums to drum in our personal spirit helpers.

The thing that amazed me about the similarities of this ceremony to the others is that Gretchen was trained in shamanism by a medicine man in Africa. The opening of the circle ceremony she used was a compilation of such ceremonies from tribal traditions all over the world. The opening ceremonies I know of are similar in intent and content in different cultures on at least three continents; Wicca paganism in Europe, Lakota religious practice in North America, and tribal shamanism in Africa. I cannot offer an explanation, but it gives me food for thought.

Over the years that I participated in the drum circle at Visions and Dreams many interesting experiences were given to me. We danced our totem animals, danced our bones in a dismemberment journey, and traveled in pairs to see if we could connect on the astral planes.

Dancing my totem animal was always fun for me. Because the group met on Saturday afternoons we wore bandanas over our eyes to keep the light out. On the journeys when we danced we wore either gauzy, lace or fringed see-through eye coverings so we wouldn't fall over things or each other while we remained in an altered state. The leader drummed for us during the entire journey. Sometimes there were two drummers.

I remember dancing black panther power. As usual, the journey started with us on the floor. Everyone except myself was lying flat on his back on the floor around a central altar. I preferred sitting cross-legged. The altar was symbolic of our spiritual intent, but was not religious in nature. Usually, there was at least one candle, animal figures and unusual stones. Sometimes, attendees brought in personal items that held meaning for them. When the drumming started I used my normal means of ascending to the astral plane. The leader did not guide us. This group was not for beginners and everyone had his way of leaving his body.

I met Joel, my guide. He or Lilly, my other guide, was always with me when I opened my channel. Panther came to me. I saw her before me, eyes flashing with life force as she watched me. Her energy leaped into me, and I vibrated with her cat essence. Rising from the pillow where I sat, I stretched with smooth feline movements, and paced along the floor. Panther's power and grace flowed through my limbs. Through the lace kerchief covering my eyes, showed the shadowy images of the other dancers and the candlelit altar. Drumbeats paced my steps. When the drumbeats changed rhythm to signal the impending end to the journey I released panther, and returned to my pillow.

In this group at every meeting after astral traveling we all shared our experience one person at a time. Other members gave feedback on their thoughts, feelings, and knowledge to help each other understand our journey. There were many people like myself who astral traveled, but not necessarily in the Shamanic tradition. We were free to express ourselves no matter our belief system.

One of the other types of journey we did was the dismemberment journey. A dismemberment journey is for spiritual and emotional cleansing, a breaking down of old unhealthy habits and beliefs, and giving oneself a fresh start. We can start such a journey with the intent or sometimes it just happens. Simply put, the flesh and organs are stripped from the bones until the bones are bare. There are many methods of cleansing; burning in fire, eaten by wild animals or birds or insects, worn away with water or by many other methods. As gruesome and painful as it may seem to the uninitiated, the actuality is quite painless and freeing.

We started the dismemberment journey in the usual way with me sitting cross-legged on the floor, the black lace bandana covering my eyes. After ascending into the astral, I asked Joel to help me with the dismemberment process. As a person who channels light the energy flowing through me and out of my hands felt normal. I waited for the process of stripping my bones to begin, expecting flesh eating animals or birds until I realized I was on fire. The energy flowing through my body was consuming my flesh. I felt heat, the same heat I usually feel when I call in the light. Yet my flesh was melting away. Of the four metaphysical elements of the universe: air, water, earth, and fire, my closest affinity is to the element of fire. It raged through me, and I was joyfully one with it. The flames receded then finally disappeared. I felt light, unencumbered, emotionally as well as physically. My old constraints of fears, unfulfilled hopes and other people's expectations of me were gone.

Through the lace bandana I glimpsed people dancing in a loose-limbed trance. This is called dancing your bones. Your flesh is gone along with your emotional baggage and you dance your freedom. Rising to my feet, I joined them, my arms and legs feeling light and fleshless, the joints barely connected. My hands dangled. I moved to the drumbeat, awkward and tentative at first. Then I felt light, fresh, and clean. The future spread out in my mind's eye like a promising green meadow. New organs and muscles grew back on my frame as I moved. Skin formed over it, starting from the top of my head, and ending at my feet. I was whole again, ready for a new start. I heard the drum signal the end of the journey. Returning to a sitting position, I came back to earth, feeling renewed and refreshed.

At one of the afternoon Shamanic Journey groups I was allowed to run an experiment with its members. Gretchen no longer led the group, and was not present. Jim had taken over and he was there. There were only six of us that day so the energy in the room had an intimate feel to it. My intent was to have us astral travel in pairs like Ruth and I did, and see if they could make a connection on the spirit plane. Although we had been meeting once a month for a few years, some of us for a shorter time, most of us did not know each other personally.

I was given free rein to do whatever I chose, be it Shamanic or otherwise. I decided to teach them my method of astral travel. First we split up into three teams of two. The partners sat cross-legged on the floor facing each other, and holding the other person's hands. Before we began I instructed them to call in their totem animal, and stay aware of their partner.

Using the steps from earlier in this book, I led everyone to the astral plane. Once we called in our totems I left everyone on his or her own, and concentrated on my journey with my partner Marianne. She and I had done some psychic work together before, but not with totems. Although we knew we had a connection neither of us had a clue what would happen on this journey. A vision of three black figures walking side by side down a country road came to me. One form was a female person wearing a pointed black witch's hat and long dark robe. Marianne was Wiccan so the clothing was no surprise to me. The second form was a huge crow sitting on her shoulder. Next to them walked a black panther. Obviously that was myself. Everyone in the Shamanic group knew my totem animal was Black Panther so I decided to call in my second totem to see if Marianne would pick up on it. Beaver showed itself in a creek, working feverishly with twigs and branches. I held the image, reinforcing its energy to give Marianne time to latch onto it. Eventually the scene faded, and Joel let me know it was time to bring everyone back to the physical plane. I hummed as I did when journeying with Ruth, then told everyone to shut down his chakras, and ground himself before opening his eyes.

Now it was time to discuss our journeys. Vansel and Barbara, who did not know one another personally, were paired together. They told of their experiences first. Barbara was surprised that Vansel saw her deer. She had rarely been to the same meetings as Vansel, and had not mentioned her totem in his presence. His lion totem being recognized by Barbara was more understandable. Vansel spoke often of his lion appearing in his journeys.

Jim and Criselda were good friends, and had meditated many times together. On this day, Jim told of flying with Criselda's eagle. That was no surprise. On the other hand everyone knew that Jim's primary totem animal was Bear. We were all caught unaware when Jim talked about feeling stationery, like he was rooted in the earth. His bear was not present. Criselda said, "That's because you were a tree." Jim laughed. He had been exploring tree energy for the previous month, melding his energy with that of trees. She had synced into Jim's tree bonding.

Marianne's experience with me was a revelation. While I saw her crow she initially saw my panther. When that animal disappeared she could not understand all the crazy work energy exuding from me, and water everywhere. Marianne had seen my symbols for Beaver without seeing the animal. It made perfect sense to her when I told her Beaver is also my totem animal.

We were all astounded at how each of us had sensed in some form the images created by his or her partner. Everyone knew such a thing existed. They just had not realized that they were able to experience it, and so could everyone else in the room.

When we were finished with the business of the circle we closed it as we always did by standing in a circle, holding hands and thanking all the spirits, teachers, and totem animals that had come to help us. Then we gave thanks to each other for the loving energy we brought to the circle, and sent our love out to the world. We disengaged our hands and the circle was closed.

CHAPTER THREE

THE OLD WOMAN IN THE CABIN

JOURNAL ENTRY
NOVEMBER 5

I hovered in the astral, meditating alone this time. My purpose was to discover a past life with my husband Carl. Wanting to look at his energy field, I concentrated on him. I soon saw part of his spirit in the astral with me. He appeared as a small being with a Chinese mask on his face, brilliantly colored in red and gold, fierce with four long teeth. I thought how fitting the mask was. Carl was drawn into himself, forever hiding his true emotions, sometimes snapping at people to keep them at bay. After twenty-six years of marriage I still did not know the inner man.

Taking his hand in mine, I flew up, but he held back, snarling at me as though ready to attack. I turned to him, and shouted for him to cut it out like a mother would to a child. He quieted, and we flew to an astral realm over rolling green meadows. We followed a narrow stream to a cabin. Smoke wafted from its stone chimney. I wanted to investigate the cabin, but Carl refused to go inside. He left me, flying off until he disappeared in the sky.

My attention returned to the little house. My curiosity was aroused, but no matter how I tried I could go no further. Feeling frustrated, I decided to return to my physical body.

I opened my eyes, and mentally adjusted to the physical plane. The mystery of the cabin haunted me. The certainty that it was a past life shared with Carl lingered with me like the scent of jasmine. Someday soon I would have to go back.

NOVEMBER 15

I saw my frozen breath fan out in front of me in the dimness of the wilderness place. My spirit was confined in the form of black panther. Dead leaves crackled beneath the pads of my paws as I loped among the winter-stripped trees. Ruth was beside me in her wolf body. The fog of her breath mingled with mine. I snarl-growled to greet her, and she howled in answer.

A man walked in front of us, the buck antlers on his head identifying him as a shaman. We followed him to a campfire, which we sat around, the leaping flames drawing my awareness into them. Panther disappeared, and I found myself in human form. Reaching around the fire to us in thought energy, it felt as though the shaman put one hand on Ruth's shoulder and his other hand on my shoulder, and spoke as in a blessing. "The circle is complete. Your destinies will now begin to come true." I felt an energy force like electricity flow through me. In the real world Ruth's clock chimed the hour like church bells, marking the words with added power. "Your destinies are one." He continued. "Go out and meet it together."

The moment seemed sacred to me, as though a universal force or God, whatever you want to call it, had touched me personally, and would send helpers to ease my way.

The surrounding energy at the campsite dissipated, and I knew it was time for us to leave that place. Yet I was not ready to return to earth. I decided to bring Ruth to where I had visited on my solo journey ten days before. Leaving Shaman behind us, we ascended, myself in the lead.

I had the sensation of flying through space. Stars whizzed past us. My physical body needed to sneeze, and having no control of it, I let it rip. The physical happening had no affect on my concentration nor did Ruth seem disturbed by it. We were not following a path or direction. I simply stated the intent to revisit the cabin in the meadow, and we were soon there after soaring over the green pasture.

This time entry into the small house was easy. Ruth followed me through the roof. We floated to the floor and looked around. The room was rustic, the furnishings simple and shabby. Although it was full daylight outside, the room was dimly lit. A woman with wide threadbare skirts down to the floor worked at the hearth where a fire crackled. She could have been a peasant of almost any century, with her drab homespun clothing. Her back was turned to us. Slowly she turned, and I saw her face. An ugly scowl disfigured her wrinkled features. I tried to understand why the woman was so angry, but mind messages from Ruth ruined my line of thought. I felt her desperate need to get the hell out of there.

Our deep-seated trust in each other is one of the underlying support beams of our friendship. I would not stay and assuage my curiosity while she was so uncomfortable. Besides, Ruth's fears might have been justified. I took her hand, and we flew from the cabin.

We did not descend to earth right away, but clung to each other as I called in The Force to surround us. Then I toned, and we returned to the physical plane.

The room was freezing! When a place is so cold for no apparent reason that could mean a disembodied spirit is present. Ruth mentioned the frigid air she had felt in the cabin, and agreed with my assumption that the old woman had followed us. We were not afraid, and decided to ignore her. After about ten minutes the room warmed without us doing anything to heat it.

We spoke of both of us being in the winter wilderness in our animal bodies, following the shaman to a campfire. Ruth was amazed that I saw her shaman. She had been astral traveling with him for years. She also experienced him stretching his arms around us, and giving us his blessing, and her clock chiming just at that moment.

Ruth was confused about where we went next. She felt it had something to do with me, but could make no sense of it. I asked her if she ever heard of the Akashic Record. When she shook her head no I explained that it is the record of all time - past, present, and future. People experience it in different ways. Some see it as a movie in a theater or on a television screen. Others see it as files in a cabinet or books in a library. It is also seen as a big book. Ruth's eyes widened.

"Yes, the big book! That's what I saw. It was huge." She held her hands above her head then spread them apart wider than her body.

"That's interesting. I've never seen the big book," I said. "Tell me about it."

Looking at me quizzically she said, "How could you not have seen the big book? It was covered with a thick layer of dust. When I blew on it to clean it off the dust came up in a cloud, and you sneezed."

The sneeze! I remembered doing it, but there was no vision of a big book. This was too bizarre to be a coincidence. Somehow I had linked into Ruth's symbol for the Akashic Record without seeing it myself. I have no explanation for this phenomenon.

Ruth told me that although she had never heard of the Akashic Record before our journey she somehow knew she was in a place of records. She also remembered flying over green fields with a quaint cabin near a stream, and coming down through the cabin's roof. Her recollection of the old woman coincided with mine. She feared that the old woman wanted to hurt me in some way, and Ruth wanted to leave. That was the emotion of hers I picked up when I decided to return to the physical plane.

We had astral traveled together again, with intention this time. Last week's experience was not a fluke. Ruth and I have decided to continue with our journeys to see where they lead us.

AKASHIC RECORD

Everything that ever happened in the past, is happening now, and will happen in the future is written in the Akashic Record. Since we have free will, and can avoid certain occurrences while creating new ones not in the plan or not living up to our potential, the future record is only probability, and subject to change.

Out-of-body travelers may see the record in different ways. It is not made of physical matter so the information is open to interpretation by our earthbound senses. What we see is merely a symbol. Some people see it as a huge book in similar proportion an ant would see a three-ring binder. Others see it as going to the movies, sitting in front of a huge screen, and watching lives happen. Another way is to become part of the picture while speaking the words, and feeling the sensations and emotions. There are any number of combinations of the above methods, and probably many vastly different other ways as well.

Most religions accept the concept of life's energy or a person's soul continuing to exist after the death of its body. There is quite a bit of controversy over what happens to the soul when it is freed from the body. The Christian view is of heaven and hell, and perhaps purgatory. In this belief system the soul does not return to Earth to live and die again. Some Eastern religions like Hindu and Buddhism are founded on the premise of reincarnation. In this case the soul returns to earth to live different lives again and again. The Akashic Record depends on the premise of reincarnation. Energy from each life exists in the astral planes in the record. Visiting the record by astral traveling and seeing or reenacting one of our lives is called past life regression.

Sometimes we visit the Akashic Record unintentionally as in the case of my first visit to the cabin in the meadow. I was astral traveling, and my husband's spirit led me there. Other times we can go there with intent like when I took Ruth to the cabin. Also we can lead other people to the record without going there ourselves as when one person hypnotizes another.

The first time I participated in a past life regression led by a hypnotist it was done afterhours at a bookstore I owned. The shop was closed, and five of us were in a sitting area at the back of the shop. A lady named Jane took us on our journey. She started with the classic hypnotic process, relaxing each part of the body. We were then given the visual impression of an elevator, and told to enter it.

I remember the metal on metal click as the door closed, and the gears grinding as the elevator took me up, up, up… to the count of six. Jane helped us all ascend at the same time, and had us open the door and step out, not into a high place, but into a different dimension. Then each of us was in her own past life. Jane helped each of us in turn, asking questions to lead us forward. My journey progressed for a while before it was my turn for Jane to come to me.

I entered a place with trees and crude wooden huts. I was a young woman. There was a man maybe a little older than I. His coloring was light, both hair and skin. We were dressed in eighteenth century clothing of poor quality and well worn. The man's name was Stephen, and I felt his gentle love envelope me. The feeling was so beautiful I almost cried. Knowledge came to me that although Stephen had been with me in many lives, he had not and would not be with me in this present life. In that time we were in an early settlement in a southern state, possibly Georgia.

Then Jane came to me in the real world. It was my turn for her to help me see and understand my journey. I told her where I was and who was with me. Fevered heat permeated my body in that life, and I felt ill as though I were dieing. Stephen was crying and holding my hand. A young female friend of mine was also there, kneeling beside me as I lay in my low bed. I told her and Stephen to take care of each other. Then I died. I remember the feeling of my soul leaving my body.

At that time Jane called everyone in the room to follow her back to awareness. We entered our elevator, and descended to earth. She counted backward as we grounded ourselves.

Since that first past life regression where someone hypnotized me, I have learned to guide others in the experience. My method differs from Jane's in many ways. Basically, Jane used a straightforward hypnotic method. There was no setting of the subject's intent for the journey or attempt to help anyone interpret the images. The way I do it is more personal and metaphysical in nature.

Before starting to put the subject in a hypnotic state, we discuss the purpose of the journey. Does the person want to know about a past life shared with someone he or she has a relationship with now? Does the person have a recurring situation or problem that suggests a karmic root? Is there an unexplained interest in or connection with a foreign culture or historical time period or place? In my experience, if a person undergoes a past life regression without starting with an intent, a meaningful experience and interpretation are less likely to happen.

Next I use the steps of hypnotic suggestion along with the opening of the chakras to free the subject's spirit from his body, and bring it to the portal. This is the same portal as described in chapter one through which one's spirit enters the astral realm. I then instruct the person to call in his spirit guide for this journey. Usually the guide appears as a cloud of energy before it takes form. If the person has a problem making contact with the guide, I will ascend to the portal, and see what he is seeing. I can interpret what is happening, and facilitate the connection between the astral traveler and the guide. The guide might be a deceased member of the person's family, a friend or an entity with which the person is unfamiliar.

Once the connection with the guide is made, the traveler asks to be shown a past life, and given a message that will answer his question. This sets an intention for the journey. The guide flies with the person to the Akashic Record. Now the past life scene is set. As we fly down into a place that looks like real life, characters from that life appear, and significant action takes place. The traveler can ask questions of the guide for clarification. I also am in the astral, and can speak to the person and his guide. The same visual and auditory messages that the guide is showing the traveler are being shown to me. I can then help to interpret the journey, and expedite it with my inquiries and remarks. While it is possible for me to communicate with the traveler's guide I usually only speak with the traveler. That is done in my physical voice, not mind-speak. For me physical verbal communication is best when putting someone under hypnosis for a past life regression. I only use mind-speak when I go out-of-body with an experienced traveler.

When the traveler has all his questions answered or is mentally exhausted and has difficulty staying in trance, it is time to return to earth. We fly back to the portal, and thank the guide. Then I help the traveler to ground his energy.

People visit the Akashic Record for many reasons. Among them are entertainment and curiosity. A better reason for which you can access the Akashic Record is to discover what karmic events in past lives can give you insight into what is happening in your present life. Among other things, it can show you the root of recurring issues, and your karmic connections with people who are important to you. Most important, it can help you pinpoint the lessons you came down to the physical plane to learn.

CHAPTER FOUR

PANTHER AT THE FIRE CIRCLE

JOURNAL ENTRY
NOVEMBER 24

I raced across the packed snow, my panther body stretching out, leaping toward the frozen horizon. I breathed in the chill air, and tasted the tang of freedom. Wolf was at my side, her breath rasping from exertion. Together we plunged into a snow bank, and tumbled over each other like two puppies at play. Snow sprayed in every direction. Without warning, a voice sounded from above us. Shaman stood there, demanding our attention.

We followed him to a huge lake, its surface like black glass in the moonlight. He pointed to an island lit with a campfire. We leaped into the frigid water, and made for the island. Ruth and I swam side by side, still in our animal forms. Water splashed out from my big paws, and sometimes closed over my head.

As we bounded onto the tiny island, dripping and shaking the wetness from our coats, a young Native American man arrived to greet us. I had the impression he was psychically on my level, not far more advanced than I, as the Shaman was.

He led us to the fire, where other animals and beings I did not recognize sat in a circle around the flickering light. The strange members of the campfire council reminded me of the cast from a science fiction movie. I received only

25

brief, partial impressions of the beings around the campfire. Some I recognized as human or Earth animals. Others had many eyes or bodies shaped in ways I had never seen before. There were furry beings and hairless creatures, and still others were birdlike. It seemed to me they were representatives from places throughout the universe, including different dimensions. As Ruth and I were in animal form, which was not our physical earthbound form, the group members might also have a different form in another place or dimension.

The Native American man invited us to join the group. He said, "It is now time to meet others like yourselves." I understood that he meant they were astral travelers like Ruth and I. Before I could focus on the others in the circle, a flame leaped from the campfire, and burned through my body. The flame expanded and consumed me, but there was no pain. I heard many voices intone a blessing of purification, and welcoming us into the union of spirits joined around the fire.

After the flames left me, I saw a gigantic bird with dark feathers sticking out at odd angles. He beckoned Ruth and I to come with him. I did not feel threatened by him, and was intrigued with the invitation. But Ruth did not want to go, and I would not leave without her.

Ruth and I knew it was time to leave the island, and together we flew into the night sky. Our animal bodies had been shed, and we were now in human form. We flew for a short while among the stars before closing in on an asteroid. We entered through what appeared to be a cave-like opening. It was like entering the center of a gigantic geode with long, glittering crystals aiming toward the center. As we hovered inside the hollow space, energy beamed at us from the crystal points. I felt exhilarated, bathing in the powerful, concentrated force. After a short while we decided to continue our journey.

Again we headed into deep space. I decided to bring Ruth to a place in the Akashic Record I had visited alone two weeks before. We landed in a forest glade in full daylight. The last time I was there I had been in the body of a young man, and had been waiting for someone. I did not know whom. No one had come, and I hoped now that whoever it was would show up. I thought Ruth might be able to help me identify the person and the purpose of the visit. While Ruth and I waited I sensed a female spirit with us in the glade. I did not see her shape, but recognized her energy as the guide who had shown me the way to this past life in the Akashic Record those weeks ago. She was not the person I was waiting for. Ruth did not see the spirit and grew impatient to leave. I knew it was time to go back to the earth plane, and hummed the signal.

Tonight my journey seemed disjointed, like dream sequences with images popping in and out, and scenes changing without warning. Some of the images were so brief and intangible that I doubted seeing them at all. Ruth told me that she experienced a lot of mind chatter tonight, and received only short impressions of places, feelings, and the presence of other beings. At first, we both doubted we had been traveling together. Then we each gave details of our island campfire meeting experiences, including the alien beings and huge bird. Our impressions were identical. Ruth also remembered playing in the snow in our animal forms, meeting Shaman, the crystal cave, and our stop in the forest. We were amazed when we verified so many of the same details.

The diversity of the travelers around the campfire caused me to ponder from where they might have come, and what is out there on the astral planes.

THE ASTRAL DIMENSION

There are many different concepts of the spirit world. Each religion has its own set of beliefs on the subject. Christians believe in heaven above and hell below. Catholics add in purgatory. Native Americans have the three worlds – the spirit world for humans, which is above in the sky, Earth, which is where we live, and below, inside the Earth where the essence of animal spirits reside. Nicheren Buddhism, the kind of Buddhism I adhere to, puts forth the afterworld as consisting of ten levels. The lower levels are for less enlightened souls, and graduating to those more enlightened, with perfection on the top.

In metaphysics there are said to be seven planes. Each plane has its own speed of vibrations. You might remember in an earlier chapter I mentioned the difference between the material earth plane and the astral plane as being a difference in the frequency of vibrations. When we raise the rate of our aura's vibrations, we can reach the next astral plane. Think of the system as though it were a freeway for automobiles. It has seven lanes. Each lane travels at a different speed. Let us pretend that a new soul enters into the right hand lane, the slowest. When the soul evolves, causing it to vibrate faster it moves into the next faster lane to the left. That is what happens when we astral travel. The physical plane is arguably on the slowest plane.

There are different schools of thought as to how many planes there are, what is on each plane, and what they are called. Aside from books I read and classes I attended, I also gained knowledge from astral traveling and channeling. Some of what I was taught in books and classes explained my experiences in the astral, and fit in with what I consider to be true. Some of it did not fit in. I kept what rang true, and disregarded that which did not. That does not mean the disregarded teachings were wrong. It means they were not in my experience. Some day I might have cause to reconsider. My concept of the astral universe is still developing as I gain experience.

Let us return to the freeway. Souls reside in a lane of speed according to their evolvement. The higher the soul has evolved, the higher the speed of the lane it resides on. The physical plane is a school where souls go to learn lessons so they can evolve, and work out karma with other souls. Souls from all lanes can have lives on the physical plane. When we successfully learn our life lessons our soul evolves and our vibration goes faster. We then move to the next faster freeway lane. We do not have to stay in the same lane to which we have evolved. When we behave in a more evolved manner, we can move temporarily to a faster lane. Likewise, when we make mistakes, we move to a slower lane for a time.

I recently astral traveled to discover what existence is like in the spirit world. What does the place of souls look like? What do souls do? What do souls look like? There are books that describe the spirit world in terms that are like our planet Earth. I have not experienced it that way, except for the Akashic Record, which is only a shadow of the physical world. My astral journey of discovery was not what I expected. As usual, I soared through the clouds, up to the portal to the spirit world. My guide Joel met me there as well as many members of my family who had passed on. My husband Carl moved forward, and took my hand. I told him and Joel the purpose of my journey, and they led me through the doorway.

We flew through what seemed like the night sky with sparkling stars. Again I asked to see the place of souls.

"This is it," Joel answered. "We are made of energy as everything else in the universe is made of energy, even the stars. Physical places like rooms with corridors are for the physical plane. Those vibrations are very slow.

Think of a ghost, passing through walls. Ghosts are made of energy that vibrates at a faster rate than the physical plane. It can move things with its energy, but cannot support objects with its bulk. There are no physical bodies on the spirit planes. Therefore, there is no need for houses."

Joel's explanation made sense to me, but it did not satisfy my curiosity. He picked up on my unspoken desire for more information. My Overself appeared in the heavens. An Overself is the repository of all the lives lived by one soul, and is the main soul that travels in the lane in the freeway of the Astral Planes. I knew it was my Overself because I had seen it on a previous astral journey, and Joel had explained what and who it was. It had made a powerful, masculine impression. When I had asked for its name, the word "Master" had come to me in a deep, theatrical voice. I now recognized the dark, shadowy figure that was wrapped in a black cloak that I knew as Master. His figure was out among the stars. Soon images of my souls from different lives appeared ranged around Master. Some of the souls were familiar to me from journeys I had taken to the Akashic Record. Threads of light led from Master to the other souls, showing their bonds to him. Then other people's souls appeared, and arranged themselves around each of the souls from my many lives. Joel explained them as being the souls that are linked to me by karma. There was a glistening gold string attaching each of my souls to each of the souls with which I have a karmic bond. I saw many karmic bonds linking themselves to each other from one life to the next, and again to me in a magically intricate pattern.

"All things are made of energy, and are linked together by energy," Joel announced.

Then Joel led me back to the portal. My husband's spirit, which was still with me, bade me good-bye and flew away. Joel remained with me.

The intent of my journey had been to get a visual image of how the souls exist in the spirit world. Joel had given me visual impressions of how energy works, first with the astral highway, then with the karmic bond pattern. Now, at the portal, my guide read my confusion on how to present the astral universe in this chapter. His last instruction to me was, "Consider what you know to be true." He then left me, and I exited through the portal, descending to earth.

This is what I know to be true, gleaned from my experiences, reinforced with classes and reading that explained what I already had seen and done.

Starting from earth, the physical plane, when we first leave our physical body on an astral journey our etheric body lifts up from the physical body. We can see and hear what is happening on earth, but no one can see or hear us. At that time we have not yet gone up to the portal. This is called remote viewing.

I rarely do remote viewing. My interests lie more toward the Akashic Record, shamanic journeys, and medium work, but I have had experience with it. The first time I experienced remote viewing it was by accident. My husband Carl's mother Frances was dieing of cancer and was in hospice care. Carl's parents lived in Portland, Oregon as did his sister and her family. We were in Southern California. Carl's sister called on the telephone. I heard Carl's side of the conversation, and realized that Frances' disease had progressed to the point that she had about two days to live. If he wanted to say good-bye, he had to go there immediately. He was still on the phone when I went into my room to pray for her easy passing. As I sat in front of my Buddhist altar, chanting for Frances, my spirit left my body. Suddenly, my consciousness was hovering near the ceiling in a stark room. There was a hospital bed with someone in it, and my father in-law sat in a chair beside the bed. He was hunched over, and I felt his desperation. I was still chanting and praying for Frances so I concentrated my energy on her. I saw the light of her life force everywhere in the room, but not in her body. This happened many years ago, long before I knew I could astral travel, and so I could not interpret what I saw. For a while I continued to chant for Frances' peace. When I was done I returned to earth, and left my room. A few minutes later the phone rang again. My sister in-law called to tell Carl that their mother had passed away twenty minutes before. That was at the same time I had seen her energy spread around the hospice room, but not in her body. I immediately understood that I had seen her pass away. It had not occurred to me before because I was inexperienced, and I thought she had two more days to live.

While I am on the subject, let me clarify the link between my Buddhist chanting and astral journeys. I am a member of the Nicheren sect of Buddhism as practiced by the Soka Gakkai organization. The sect does not teach astral travel in any way. It is something that happens to me while chanting because of my psychic abilities. The chanting raises my vibrations in a similar way that opening the chakras does. I chant to pray for help for myself and other people, not to astral travel. Chanting still sends me out of my body, but I do not go through the portal, and I concentrate on the prayer. Most people do not go out-of-body while chanting.

Many years ago when I was taking classes at the Learning Light Foundation I took part in an ongoing group to investigate astral travel. The group was mainly focused on remote viewing. Judy, who led the group, usually took us on a guided journey. A guided journey is when a person has an astral journey with someone else telling him how to leave the physical plane, where to go, what to see, and what to do. There are also recordings that do the same thing. I am usually not impressed with guided journeys. Those experiences share many aspects in common with hypnotic suggestion. Someone not acquainted with astral travel would not know if he were truly out-of-body or merely hypnotized, accepting the speaker's suggestions. At the time of the investigation group I was an experienced traveler, did not need Judy's instructions, and preferred to do it myself. Judy's instructions felt very confining, but they kept me grounded to this side of the portal, which was new for me.

On one investigation group journey Judy instructed us to leave our body, and fly through the early evening sky to Disneyland. The Learning Light Foundation is in the city of Anaheim only a few miles from the amusement park. Everyone in the group had been there in the physical on at least one occasion. I had not visited Disneyland in many years. She directed us to soar over the rooftops to the main entrance. My awareness was concentrated on my own journey, and I paid no attention to the others in my group. Judy did not ask us to think about what anyone else in the group was doing.

The images of Disneyland's Main Street at dusk were magical, lit up with its turn of the twentieth century charm. Following our leader's instructions, I flew over Main Street into Fantasy Land and found the carousel. It was not one of my favorite rides, but in the interests of the experiment I chose a horse. It was already occupied by a little girl who was about five years old, but the carousel was full of passengers, and there was no other choice. I sent soothing energy to her so she would not sense me, and be disturbed. Her delight with the ride seeped from her to me. As we went around, I felt the wind go through my astral body. There was no feeling of the horse under me, although I kept up with the undulating rhythm. The scenery as it moved by was only a flickering impression, not a steady panorama as it would have been on the physical plane. The sensations were a surprise. I was not used to remote viewing, and did not realize it would be more like fleeting astral travel impressions, and less like the continuity of being on the physical plane.

After the ride stopped, Judy set us free to roam the park at will. There had been so many years since my last visit to Disneyland that new rides had been constructed. The one that interested me most was the one with the Raiders Of The Lost Ark theme. I had heard that attraction had different scenarios, and riders might not see the same things when going on it more than once. My impressions of the ride were short, but intense. I got onto an open car with physical people beside and behind me. The car ran along a rail, picking up speed and lurching, making rumbling sounds. We went to a chamber with snakes everywhere. From there the car went through a dark passage into a huge cavern with a fire pit. We fell down into the burning pit. The car went careening out of control through a cave, and spewed out into fresh air as the ride ended. It occurred to me that I felt emotionally detached, not hooked into the thrill of the ride as I would have been if my physical body were experiencing it. Immediately, I found another car at the start of the ride and went through again. The second time around the car went uphill on the rails and crossed a narrow rope bridge.

Before the second ride was complete Judy called us together to return to the Learning Light Center. Each member of the group had a chance to tell about his astral experience. Another member mentioned riding on the carousel with a physical person. We had similar sensory impressions. During my turn to speak I asked if anyone had ever been on the Indiana Jones ride in the physical, so my journey could be corroborated. One woman verified the existence of the snake room, and the car lurching and running out of control. Since that night I have had the opportunity to physically experience the attraction. I recognized the lurching, rolling quality of the car, which looked like an ancient Jeep. There was also a tableau that resembled the burning pit I saw on my astral journey.

In general, my experience with remote viewing was much like my other astral travel experiences. I received only fleeting impressions of places and happenings. Other astral travelers might be more attuned to remote viewing, and see things as more solid. Remote viewing is not my forte, and I only report on my personal perceptions.

As we leave the level of remote viewings, our spirit ascends to the portal, which is the entrance to the next dimension. I have heard of, and once visited, a place in the astral called the black void. It was explained to me as a band between earth and the other side of the portal. My only personal experience with the black void happened before I had learned of it in a class at the Learning Light Foundation. I was meditating alone at home, and had just started the session. The images of stars, impressions of golden energy, and the sensation of flying that I usually equated with entering the astral planes did not come to me. I asked for the white light to show itself, but it did not. Fear is not a normal response from me when I am out-of-body, but this time my nerves were jittery. There was not a speck of light. The darkness was oppressive. I felt stuck, and could not get out. Usually, all I have to do is think of going somewhere when I am astral traveling and I am there, but this time it did not work. I was trapped. This happened before I learned to communicate with my guides, so calling for help did not occur to me. I decided to fly as fast as I could to get somewhere else, but it was like traveling in a closed elevator. There was nothing to see to gauge how fast or in what direction I was going. The thought went through my mind to open my physical eyes, and come back to earth, sort of pulling the plug on a malfunctioning machine. Then I saw stars, felt myself flying, and sighed in relief. I was out of that frightening place, and have never returned.

The beings that Wolf and Panther encountered around the campfire on the island suggest the existence of many planets and dimensions. These beings have lives in their respective civilizations so they can learn lessons, evolve to higher energy frequencies, and work out karma with other souls. The size of the astral planes is vast; some people say it is endless. There is no map I know of that shows every place in it, and where each place is. I have mentioned only a paltry few that I have experienced. There is much more out there to be explored.

CHAPTER FIVE

THE FOREST REVISITED

JOURNAL ENTRY
DECEMBER 17

Ruth is working crazy hours so I am on my own for a while. I meditated on my patio in the sun. It was cool, but the California sunshine baked into my body, filling me with the universal force.

Within a couple of minutes I left this plane and ascended to the small forest glade where I had taken Ruth on our last journey. The late afternoon sun shone through the swaying branches of trees high overhead. I heard the crackle of leaves brushing against each other and the call of birds. I waited there in the form of a young man, willing the mystery spirit to come to me From out of the forest a girl in her mid-teens emerged. She wore a dress of tanned animal skins, and her black hair was loose and straight, down to her waist. Her complexion was tan as was my own. She was petite and lovely.

Love for her rushed through me, and settled in my loins. I knew I would not be able to think rationally if I allowed his emotions to cloud my mind. Stepping out of his body, I backed away to the edge of the glade and watched.

They embraced. He was eager, exuberant, vital, while she was timid and shy. They whispered love words to each other. I did not hear what they said, but the meaning was clear. Yet all was not well. Fear and sadness surrounded the girl like a billowing black cloud.

When the young man tried to bring her to his boat on the riverbank she refused to go. He insisted and she fought him off. I felt her panic, and tried to stop him. They did not know I was there, and I had no physical capabilities, but I sent my energy in a message to him. I do not know if he stopped on his own or if it was because of my action. At any rate, he let go of her, and she soon left the glade.

Although the man was still a puzzle to me, I had seen enough for this visit. There was much to digest, but I put off dissecting it until later, when I would return to the physical plane. I flew up and away from the forest, not yet ready to come back to the earth plane.

The cave Ruth and I had seen had intrigued me, and I went there now. It was dark and spooky at the mouth of the cave. Eerie echoes bounced off the walls, and I wondered what manner of beasts might lurk inside. But my adventurous spirit won out. After all, what could a beast do to me? I had no physical body to damage. As I was about to fly in, something yowled and thumped my back down on the earth plane.

My silver cord reeled me back, and I crash-landed with a thunk. I opened my eyes to see Sammy, my neighbor's Siamese cat, directly behind me. His yowl and the thump of his tail had brought me back. This dumbfounded me. Sammy is in the habit of attacking my cat, and I always chase him from my yard. When he sees me he runs. I took his uncharacteristic behavior as a rescue by a guide from danger in the cave.

After a little while, I settled down again, and left my body. I was under salt water, swimming up to the surface, in the form of the same young man from the forest. Fresh air burned into my lungs as my head came out of the water. My masculine, powerful body felt glorious as I swam to a nearby island.

A young, male friend waited for me there. He teased me about my ladylove, and my fear of her father. I wanted to ask her father for permission to marry her, but he would not accept me. Further clarification was blocked, and I had trouble concentrating. I decided to end this astral trip, and return to my body.

Awakening on the patio, I sat there in contemplation. My incarnation as a young man held an illusive significance for me. His relationship with the woman was a karmic cause of an important bond in my present life, but my guides are keeping me from discovering what it is. It is not yet time to piece things together.

JOURNAL ENTRY
DECEMBER 31

The initial purpose of this meditation was to send energy to my projects, and bless my family and others for the new year. I did this, and then went out of my body.

I found myself in a hut. It was night and I lay in the dark, but I knew the hut had a domed roof, and was in a village. I was inside the physical form of the young man from the forest. Beside me, in my arms, lay the woman from the glade. We had been making love, and I was in a good humor, sated and drowsy. She, on the other hand, was nervous, frightened of someone discovering us. Her fear made me uncomfortable, and with stealth I left her village. Once in the forest my form returned to the cloud-like astral body. I took off for a destination unknown...

I received the distinct impression that the young man was from a different society from his lover, and that was where their problem originated. His cabin and boat were European fashion, yet his appearance was almost as dark as the woman's. I think his heritage was half from her race and half from the white man's world. But he was not of her tribe.

This past life haunts me, and I am drawn to it more with each visit. What lesson is in it for me, and how will knowledge of it change my life?

REINCARNATION

In general, people of the Western religions have a backwards idea about reincarnation. In their concept the earth plane is the real world, and death is just a place where we float around in the dark until we get back to earth, a sort of purgatory with no hope of heaven. In truth, for Buddhists the return to earth is not the main goal, but rather a necessary milestone in a much more important journey.

Consider your soul as a spark of energy flung out from the central core of the universal force. More than anything you want to return to that glorious place that mothered you, but first you must improve yourself, and rise to that level of vibration. You must burn out your impurities, intensify your light, and glow brighter and hotter than you could ever imagine. After eons of struggle and learning you will evolve to the highest vibration, and rejoin the ultimate energy source.

But how does your small spark evolve into a steady flame? The key is to learn to live in harmony with the universe, in your case that includes people on the physical plane. There are other worlds in this dimension, and other planes where sparks can evolve, but a soul usually stays with the same planet for purposes of karma.

Souls between lives do not have the strong, uncontrollable emotions and passions that a physical body contributes through its genes. Nor do they have desires of the flesh or social conditions where human foibles can be acted out. In other words, there is no temptation or opportunity to do good deeds. It is easy for a man marooned on a desert island to live a chaste life in which he knows no greed or jealousy, and hurts no one. It is easy to be good when there is no opportunity to do otherwise. Likewise, there are few experiences from which to learn. In essence, there are limited challenges in the spirit world.

There are entities in the spirit world called oversouls, also known as overselves. Each oversoul is the main repository for the knowledge culled from experiences during its lives on the physical plane. While each life continues to exist in the Akashic Record, that life is only a record, and not the real thing. Only a part of the oversoul is sent down to the earth plane to learn a lesson.

Consider the earth plane as a school for souls. When the oversoul is ready to send a part of itself to the physical plane to learn another lesson it consults with its guides, and they all decide which life lessons to work on, karma to continue with other souls, and the life situation that will best suit its needs. The oversoul remains in the spirit world, while a part of its soul descends to the earth plane.

One afternoon I was astral traveling with Nila, who was a fellow psychic reader in a metaphysical shop where I worked. We were sitting on chairs on my patio, holding hands as we left our body. Our intent was to astral travel together although we had no plans or destination in mind.

I was nervous about astral traveling with Nila. Her gifts were so much more highly developed than mine, and in such a different direction that I had serious doubts whether we would make contact with each other out there. Although Nila was born into a Christian home, she had been practicing Wicca for many years. Also, her husband practiced shamanism, and she was familiar with that belief system as well. At the time of this particular astral journey my knowledge of shamanism was very limited. I felt at a disadvantage.

This journey occurred a few years after my initial experiences with Ruth, and I had advanced to traveling with my guide Joel. He joined me, and together with Nila we embarked on our adventure.

My first impression was of me sitting at the same council fire surrounded with otherworldly souls as I had visited with Ruth. A huge bird that Ruth and I had met before at the council rose from the fire. On its back it transported us to the back alleyways of an old European city. I got the feeling it was London or Paris in the late 1800's. The aura of hopeless destitution permeated the street. There was darkness of night with no lamplights or flicker of candles. Everything was in the shadows of squalid brick and wood buildings. The stench of rotting food, feces, and dead things clogged the air. A tall man in a stovepipe hat and black cape stood in front of us. I felt an intimidating power wafting from him. I recognized the dark form and his energy as the entity I knew as "Master". It was my oversoul. No matter how I tried to contact him, there was no interaction between myself and Master. I could go no further, and knew it was time for Nila and myself to end the journey. My humming signaled my desire to return to earth.

Nila's account of her journey held startling similarities to mine. She also filled in details that I had not experienced. The similarities were so profound that I had no doubt the parts of her visions, which were not the same as mine, were true as well.

She spoke of sitting on a council of seven souls that coincides time-wise, and with the same functionality as my council of extraterrestrial beings around the campfire. An ancient being, a wise man we had known for eons, stood up. He joined us, and together we flew out into the universe with him as our guide. I took this wise man as Nila's symbol for the energy I knew as the huge bird.

She also visited the streets of old London or Paris. The words she used to describe it were "the red light section of the city", meaning a poor, sordid, vice-ridden part of town. Her vision was of our backs walking down the street at night.

"Who was the big, tall man looming over you?" she asked me. "It was a dark, stern, powerful presence. He was there for you. Who was he?"

I told her he was my oversoul.

"Ah. That makes sense," she said. Then Nila told me about a small child she had found in that alley, a child who had been abandoned to die, but was not dead. A Star of David had glowed in a hidden corner of the alley, and that was where she had found the toddler. The Star of David was her symbol that the child was connected to me in some way. Nila had picked up the little girl, and handed it to Master. He took her in his arms, and bowed in acceptance. She then heard my signal to return to Earth.

I had not seen the child in my journey, and was curious about it. A few days later I channeled my guide Joel, and asked the significance of Nila's journey, who the child was, and why it had been given it to Master. Joel said that Nila had performed a psychic rescue. The child had died, but its spirit had not returned to join with the oversoul. It haunted the streets of that old city. Nila had helped the energy of the child to rejoin its oversoul, which happened to be the same oversoul as mine. In that way the child and I are connected. We share the same oversoul.

The level of evolution of one of an oversoul's lives on earth does not reflect in that life's material circumstances. Just because it may have monetary wealth and a loving family situation in a life does not mean the easy life was earned from doing good deeds in previous lives. Let us return to the concept of life on earth as a school for souls. When an oversoul meets with its guides to determine its karma for our prospective life it decides which lessons it will work on. The oversoul might be learning to overcome adversity such as being physically handicapped or being born to poverty in a third world nation where mere survival is a colossal challenge. Such difficult lives are not necessarily punishment for missteps in past lives, but opportunities for growth.

I am aware of seven of my oversoul's incarnations, including my present life. Let us consider the situations and karmic lessons he chose to learn in those lives. It would help us to look at them in the order of their historical occurrence to notice the correlations between the aim of the life lessons and the circumstances of that incarnation.

The first of my oversoul's lives under examination was discovered by me on an astral journey I had with Nila. My first impression on this journey was of descending into a sea with air bubbles rising around me. Sinking into the water lasted so long that I wondered why it was taking so much time to reach my destination. For myself and many other astral travelers moving through water means going from one place to another or traveling through time. Nila also started by descending in water, but saw an image of the god Neptune with his long beard and metal trident. This led her to believe we were literally under the sea.

When we finally reached our destination I saw columned halls such as in ancient Greece. Nila also saw the columned halls, but thought we were in Atlantis, the long ago city believed by some people to have sunk beneath the sea. Atlantis is one of those proposed things that are not in my experience. I do not outright deny its existence. It just is not part of my belief system at this time. Wherever Nila and I were, ancient Greece or Atlantis, we were there together.

I got the impression of intense spirituality and scientific knowledge. I knew myself to be a male scientist. My knowledge was so advanced and profound that it was symbolized by a brilliant light that I felt as a powerful physical energy. At one point I tried to send this energy to Nila in a mind message.

As I was ready to leave the hall, a guide that I experienced as made of light took me up above the Earth so I could see the entire planet from space, the continents and seas lit by the sun. Then we were descending to Earth, and continued down inside the earth. I felt no impact as my astral body came in contact with the planet. I continued to descend into the heart of the Earth.

Nila also saw us as very advanced scientists, but her concept was more detailed than mine. In her interpretation we were scientists together in Atlantis, trying to save our homeland from the polar shift. She saw a red crystal, which to her was the symbol for the abuse of great knowledge. She received information from me telepathically, which I remember sending to her in the form of energy. At the end, Nila also remembered an escort taking her down to the underworld. She understood this to mean death.

Recently, I channeled my guide Joel to ask him about the life lesson Master wanted worked on during the incarnation concerning the scientist in the columned halls. The word HUMILITY lit up in neon lights. The scientist was very arrogant, prideful of his intelligence and ability to communicate telepathically. He thought he could accomplish anything. Ultimately, his research failed, and he died like any other man. More to the point, he did not grow as a human being, did not learn the lesson of humility.

When I am describing a past life regression I use the first person "I" because I am physically experiencing the sensations. I use the third person "he or she" when later discussing this life. Rather than thinking of the incarnations as my own past lives, they more accurately are a part of my oversoul's lives.

The second of Master's incarnations we will look at also involves Nila. As you may recall, in a past chapter I mentioned an astral journey Nila and I shared that we saw our symbols for Egypt. I saw Horus, the form of a man with the head of a bird, and she saw the Pyramids. On that trip we both saw hundreds of campfires across the land. It was night, and we did not see much other than the fires, but we knew this was an encampment of an ancient Roman army. At the beginning we saw two men in long dark robes, men of wisdom and spiritual power. We both saw them, but knew we were not incarnated in their lives. I perceived myself in that time period as a young servant, and Nila as a woman a little older than myself. Nila saw us as two young females sitting beside the road with Roman soldiers passing in front of us, tossing coins to us. We got up, and danced down the road behind the Romans. When I asked Nila whether she saw us as camp followers, she was less diplomatic about it. She said to her the gold coins meant we were prostitutes.

Later that same day we journeyed again, and returned for a short time to that same life. Nila saw the two black-robed men and two women with the Roman army, but she could not see further details of that life. My experience on this journey was more enlightening than Nila's. I also saw the two women. At first they followed the Roman army. In the next scene they were cavorting with high-ranking soldiers in a Roman bath. We, as the women, were spies, and sold the information we gleaned from the soldiers to the two black-robed men.

Recently I channeled my guide Joel to discover Master's purpose in that incarnation. The word SURVIVAL came to me. The two Egyptian women were alone and unprotected in a brutal men's society. They were downtrodden and humiliated by Egyptians and Romans alike. All men took advantage of them, and they felt no loyalty to any man. There was no malicious or avaricious motive behind their dealings. Everything they did was done as a means for survival. This life was also an exercise in humiliation.

The next life we will look at is one where I was a medieval monk sometime during the fourteenth century. It first revealed itself to me during a solo visit to the Akashic Record. At that time I was inside a huge cathedral with enormous stained-glass windows. I was one of many dark-robed monks praying on their knees.

A few months later Ruth and I took an astral journey to that same cathedral. We both saw ourselves as monks which validated my prior journey to this place. Our spiritual bond in that life was similar to the one we have in this life. We astral traveled together, and channeled spirits. If we had been discovered doing these activities, we would have been burned or hanged as heretics. The fourteenth century came to my mind because I saw myself dieing of the Black Plague, a historical occurrence that happened in the mid-thirteen hundreds.

A solo journey for clarification for the purpose of the monk's life gave me unexpected insight into that life and my present life as well. I was a light worker then, as I am now. A light worker is someone who can use the universal force to create good. As a monk, Master learned to use his talents within the Church's system, an endeavor that was difficult and dangerous. The monastic, prayerful life was the only one he could find during that era to express his spirituality. Outside the monastery, life was too difficult to live and develop spiritually. In my present life I know intuitively when and how to use my light working gifts of channeling, astral travel, and medium work without calling too much negative attention to myself. While metaphysics in this modern age in this country is frowned upon or laughed at by a majority of the population, the practice of it is not punishable by death as it was in past centuries. Master's purpose in his life as a monk was a lesson on being true to who you really are in the face of great opposition. The lesson of survival that was learned in his life in ancient Egypt while the Romans were there was very helpful in his monk's life.

The fourth incarnation under discussion involves the old woman in the cabin. My understanding puts it in the sixteenth or seventeenth century in middle Europe, maybe Germany or Poland. The old woman was not one of Master's lives, but she was a relative of his incarnation as a much younger woman.

One of my recurring visits to the Akashic Record during that time and place occurred with me coming into awareness at a town square's water well. I was a young woman, possibly fourteen years old, hauling a full bucket up from inside the well. There were two buckets of water that I fastened to a yoke, and balanced on my shoulders. Cobblestones were hard against my bare feet as I walked under the load. A horse's hooves clattered on the stones in front of me, and stopped, barring my way. I halted and looked up. A young nobleman, recognizable by the quality of his clothes and horse, grinned down at me. I stepped aside, and tried to continue on, but the horse moved to stand in my way again. This time I changed direction to get away from the horse's path, but it was there yet again. There was no denying the nobleman was detaining me deliberately. My heart thudded with panic. I would have run to safety had the burden on my shoulders not been so heavy. Suddenly the horseman laughed, and pulled his horse around to continue on his way. I shook for a few moments until my heartrate slowed. Then I hurried home.

For months I saw no connection between the cabin in the meadow and the girl at the well. Only when I was looking for karmic bonds did the relationship and its meaning become clear. But that explanation is for the chapter on karma. So you will have to wait until then.

The fifth incarnation is the one where I was a colonial woman. We will remember in chapter three I visited with her during a group past life regression led by Jane. When I channeled recently for an understanding of the meaning for that life, my impression was that the colonial woman was supposed to learn to challenge her hard existence. She did well during her short life. Even though her life, first in England then in primitive conditions in her new home was physically and emotionally taxing, her spirit was always courageous and hopeful. Another component of Master's colonial life was the loving relationship she had with her husband Stephen. The karma between her and Stephen moved forward, although they were not together for more than a few years before she died.

Also slated for the chapter on karma is part of the discussion of Master's life that I accessed as the young man in the tribal society. His dealings with the young woman he was forced to leave behind caused a karmic connection in my present life. Therefore, we will wait for the explanation in the chapter on karma.

The main purpose for the young man's incarnation was his learning to deal with alienation, being an outcast because he was half of the tribal race and half of another race, possibly Caucasian. There were very few Caucasian people in the area, so there was little choice for him. He was forced to deal with his "otherness" in the one society or live alone. During a channeling session with my guide Joel I asked about the young man's life, its purpose, and success with overcoming others' rejection of him. I was told that he became a traveling peddler, moving and trading from one tribe to another. In his later years he settled in a small community where he was marginally accepted, but he always felt apart from them, and never grew comfortable with his situation. This is the sixth incarnation I recognize as belonging to Master.

That brings me to my present life, the seventh of Master's lives of which I am aware. A few of the major challenges I have dealt with can be traced back to my past lives. My anger and struggle for self-esteem because I am a woman in a male dominated world is a holdover from as far back as the Egyptian prostitute in the Roman army camp. In my present life I left the Orthodox Jewish religion because of the low place women hold in that culture. From Master's incarnation as a medieval monk, I inherited the need to balance my metaphysical talents and affiliations in a society not accepting of my beliefs. I learned early on not to mention my Buddhist or metaphysical affiliations to people unless they bring up the subject of religion or spirituality, and someone specifically asks me a question. There is no shame or avoidance on my part, but I see no point in causing people to feel uncomfortable, myself included. If there is a discussion on metaphysics or religion that seems open to my spiritual views on an intellectual basis, I am delighted to participate.

Sometimes such conflict is unavoidable, and I have been forced to make a stand. My husband, Carl, did not let a day go by that he did not belittle or attack my belief in metaphysics. That was one of the more pressing reasons that I decided to live apart from him. Another reason for leaving him was my lives-long struggle for self-esteem that I mentioned before in reference to the life of the Egyptian prostitute.

This brings me back to my original statement about reincarnation not being based on gaining an easier life in payment for past good deeds. Although I have been blessed materially in this life, my lack of a need to struggle for subsistence has been more of a hindrance than a gift in some ways. My husband was a good provider, and for that reason I stayed with him longer than was good for my emotional and spiritual progress. Later in this life living on my own I learned more about myself and my strengths than I could have by staying in that living arrangement. When living alone, my day-to-day existence became materially less comfortable, and my free time became far more limited because I had to have a full time job, but my life lessons progressed once I left my comfort zone.

Thus we see that an easy life is not a reward, but presents a challenge. Also, as seen from the physically demanding and penniless existence of the colonial woman, a hard life is not a penance, but an opportunity to overcome difficulties and shine brighter. She never complained or gave up, and strengthened her husband with her love. Such lack of negativity accompanied by positive actions helped make her aura gain brilliance.

The point of incarnations on the earth plane is to master the lessons we are sent down here to learn. As we do so our vibrations intensify, and rise up the seven levels of the astral planes until our pure light returns home to the core of energy from which we were spawned. The process of this remarkable voyage is called reincarnation.

CHAPTER SIX

THE PUZZLES ARE SOLVED

JOURNAL ENTRY
DECEMBER 31 CONTINUED

Flying up and away from the forest, I returned to the cabin in the meadow. Thoughts of the old woman Ruth and I had seen gave me feelings of anxiety, but I was determined to discover once and for all the mystery of my karmic bond with my husband.

Hovering above the cabin, I beckoned the spirit who lived there to come to me. I expected the old crone to appear, and was surprised to see the spirit with the mask who I recognized as my husband Carl. Wordlessly, he pulled on my arm, indicating he wanted me to go with him.

"What do you want? Where are you taking me?"

As soon as the words formed in my mind, I found myself in the cabin in the meadow where he had led me before. I was in the body of a young woman, seated in a rocking chair in front of the hearth fire. An infant swaddled in threadbare cloth lay in my arms. As I looked at the baby's face, trying to identify him, I felt his emotions as though they were my own. He seemed to beg, LOVE ME! LOVE ME! His desperate need was a twisting ache in my heart. I held him to me, and rocked back and forth, crooning to calm his intense emotions. I buried my face in his blanket, and wept.

The baby was Carl, in a different body, in a different time, but Carl

46

nonetheless. We had been mother and child in this previous life, when I had abused or abandoned him; I am not sure which, a life in which I had withheld my love and affection, two things he craved from me into future centuries. Calling in the universal healing energy, I let it pass through my body and into his.

We remained in that position until my eyes dried, my spirit calmed, and I was ready to leave. As my spirit rose, and I looked behind me, I saw the old woman standing behind the rocking chair, her hand on its back, gently rocking the woman and child. She looked up at me, and smiled.

Once again in my meditation room, I grounded myself, and opened my eyes. My face was wet with tears. The force of my experience with Carl shook me to my foundation. Much about our relationship was explained by the scene in the cabin. Our Karmic bond is about giving and receiving love. No matter how hard I try to get close to Carl he keeps me at a distance. Yet he wants my affection. It is as though he protects himself against me hurting him when that is not my intention. I now know the cause was in another life. His experience was so traumatic that it created a karmic effect. Centuries later he still does not trust me.

I wanted to know what could be done in the present to help heal our relationship. The answer from my guide was. "Just love him. Touch him, and let him know you are there for him." That sounded right to me.

The interpretation of what transpired in the cabin was not a logical deduction. My guides gave it to me as a "knowing". As soon as questions came to my mind, their answers appeared with no hint of doubt. Sometimes the answers were given to me even before I had a chance to form the questions. The old woman in the cabin was a guiding spirit, one with which I was not familiar, perhaps one of Carl's. It was as though she orchestrated what happened in that room, and would not allow me to leave until I completed what she thought needed to be done.

FEBRUARY 1

It was evening, and I had fallen asleep on my sofa. When I awoke I was disoriented, and had trouble grounding, perfect circumstances for an astral journey. I sat on a pillow on the floor, set two lit candles beside me, and went out of my body.

My past life as the young man in the forest troubled me, and I wanted further understanding. Last week I had returned to the forest for a short visit, and had discovered that the woman the man had loved was pregnant with his child. This time I would not leave until I understood the message this past life held for me.

Although I meditated alone, four souls joined me on the other side, spirit guides with whom I was familiar. There was Shaman from my astral journeys with Ruth and three of my personal guides, Joel, Lilly and Leland. Never before had I seen them all at once. Their presence told me this would be a momentous occasion.

We stood in the forest, my ladylove and I, facing each other as if in conversation. Instead of waiting for the story to unfold, I questioned the guides.

"What am I to learn from this experience? This woman was to have my child. What happened in my relationship with her?" I asked.

The answer came from one of the guides, Shaman I think. "Both she and you were afraid to face the consequences of your love. Her father would be furious and likely kill you. Fearing for your life, she begged you to leave, but she refused to leave her family. You climbed in your boat and went far away, leaving her to her fate alone. She lived in disgrace. The child did not live to manhood. He died at six or seven years old."

One of my burdens in this life is taking on guilt whether it is rightfully mine or not. My first interpretation of her situation in that life came from that place of guilt. I thought I must face my life squarely, do what I know in my heart is right, no matter the result. I should have stayed with her, and not run off to save myself.

"Who is she?" I asked. "Which person in my present life?"

"Your mother," came the answer. "The issue you and she were together in this life to work on is guilt. You blamed yourself for leaving her behind in New York when you and your husband moved to California, then blamed yourself again years later when she was ill, and you had to leave her in the care of your brother. Consider the issue in your past life and in this one."

Ah yes, guilt. She was a grand master at inflicting it on me as Jewish mothers are famous for doing. And I accepted every bit she offered to me, and added my own portion on top of that. She played a game of push me-pull me. Once when I wanted to fly to New York to visit her, she told me not to come, then blamed me for staying away.

The guide continued, "In that past life your young woman had the choice to leave with you, but she would not. With that decision she put her life and that of her child in jeopardy. That guilt should have been hers. If you had stayed with her and been killed, it would have served no one. The focus of your blame should not have been for abandonment, but for lack of forethought. You should not have given her a child."

I saw into my lover's future, and felt her emotions. She walked through her village with her gaze focused on the ground at her feet. Her bitterness and martyrdom surrounded her like a rain cloud. I knew if she walked in the sunshine, she would refuse to turn her face up to the light. The resemblance of this part of her personality to my mother's was uncanny.

The pith of the lessons came to me in my guide Joel's voice. "Do not own guilt that does not belong to you. Just because someone is hurt, and says it is your fault does not make it so. The other person must carry her baggage, and not expect you to carry it for her. Also, you are not responsible for the part of someone else's karma which you do not control. Everyone must take responsibility for her own life."

Understanding how karma works, I accepted that principle, and felt wonderfully free.

I saw the energy of the guides fade. They were leaving me, and I knew this journey was done. I said my farewells to the young woman, knowing I would not see her again, and returned to Earth.

The identification of the young woman as an incarnation of my mother surprised me. I could not see the connecting thread of karma until the guides explained it to me. Then it all came clear at once. Control and manipulation were my mother's issues, and guilt was mine.

My mother passed away last year, and I saw this insight into the Akashic Record as part of my guides' attempt to give me closure. Since her death the dynamics of our mother-daughter relationship has milled around in my mind as I have tried to make sense of our chaos. Through my learning about karmic bonds, my visits to the Akashic Record, and channeling my mother's spirit the two of us have made progress toward peace with one another.

KARMA

Karma is best known to people in Western cultures as predestination. Even societies with predominant religions that do not teach reincarnation have words for it such as fate, destiny, and kismet. Another aspect of karma is reaping the consequences for our behavior, namely cause and effect. Yes, karma is both of these, and so much more.

The Eastern religions based on reincarnation sometimes vary on their teachings about karma. For example, the Hindus believe a human who led an abhorrent life can return to life as an animal. Many Buddhist sects believe people and animals are on different karmic paths, and do not cross over. Cats go to cat heaven, and reincarnate only as cats, just as people go to their own afterworld, and come back solely as people. Even different sects within a major religion may have alternate interpretations of it. No matter the differences between religious doctrines, the basics of reincarnation and karma are the same.

Karma is the proposed lesson plan for a life on earth. That does not mean everything we plan will happen. Freedom of choice is one of the most important elements in this system. We learn from our choices, if not during life, then afterward as we evaluate our actions.

When it is time for us to enter a new body, we meet in the astral with spirit guides. There we decide upon the lessons we will try to master, and the other souls with whom we will work out our tangled karmic bonds. When dealing with other souls it is payback time. This can bode well or ill for us, depending on whether our actions are positive or negative. We might be the recipients of the abuse we dealt out to a person in another life or receive a favor from someone we helped. Also, we could find ourselves in the same circumstances together as in the past life, and be given the opportunity to correct the mistake. There are countless possibilities.

In order to discover which lessons were set for me in this life I considered what were my recurring challenges through the years. First were my feelings of isolation and low self-esteem. As a child, positive reinforcement was rare in my home. My mother believed that she should not compliment me or I might get a swelled head. Although I lived in Brooklyn, New York where there were forty students in each class I had few friends, if any. And those I rarely saw. I was convinced other children disliked me. My world consisted of reading books, and an elaborate fantasy life to keep me company.

Contributing to my isolation was my feeling of being different from everyone else. Of course, we all have our personality traits, talents, and innate and cultural preferences to make us unique, but some of us have differences that cross over the line of what is thought to be normal. My fantasy world was not mentioned by me to anyone until it had not been a part of me for years. I knew it was not normal.

In fact my active imagination held me back from the knowledge that I had been astral traveling. I thought my journeys were another sort of fantasy until my journeys with Ruth. Her verification of what I was seeing gave credence to our journeys together. Since our initial in-tandem experiences I have learned to tell the differences between my imagination and bonafide astral journeys. In my experience journeys are always done in an altered state (meditation) with my body relaxed and inert. I cannot multitask while my spirit is out of my body. Electrical energy streams through me at an accelerated rate, tingling in my hands and feet. My mind is empty and at rest. Images, sounds and impressions are given to me, not created by me.

Fantasies, on the other hand, are conscious creations done while my brain is functioning at a lower energy frequency than when I am astral traveling. It is on the same energy level as daydreaming. I can do it while performing mindless tasks such as walking or cooking. Actually, my life has become so complete that I have not created a fantasy world in many years. I no longer need one to retreat from reality or fill in missing emotional spaces. My gain in self-esteem sounded the death knell for my need for fantasies.

I was thirty-eight years old, and had been battling self-esteem issues for most of my life when karma knocked on my door. Someone on the PTA board at the elementary school my son attended approached me to teach Project Self-Esteem. The Orange County Board Of Education sponsored the program under the umbrella of its Just Say No anti drug campaign. The school's program consisted of two teams of three or four volunteers each who taught scripted lessons every two weeks throughout the year. Emphasis was put on how to deal with people and situations in an appropriate and confident way. After teaching the program for five years some of what I taught must have rubbed off on me, because since then I no longer feel uncomfortable with people. In fact, I taught self-esteem as a Weight Watchers lecturer, and as a volunteer doing group discussion sessions with participants at the High Hopes Rehabilitation Center for Brain Injury Victims. Although my self-esteem is no longer lacking, the subject continues to be an important part of my life as I help others to raise theirs.

As for feeling myself different, and therefore apart from other people, I have learned to deal with that. Being different does not have to be a negative force in my life. I am a Caucasian Buddhist in a predominantly Christian society, and a metaphysical practitioner in a place where most people are disbelieving of psychic phenomena. To my surprise and relief I have found loose communities and even large organizations in some cases, where I can feel comfortable in my differentness. And of course there is the Internet where I can communicate with like-minded people. Also, I have learned to keep my unpopular beliefs private so I do not cause other people to feel uncomfortable with me.

Another karmic lesson that keeps appearing in my life is learning to stand up for myself. This topic touches on the theme of self-esteem. As a child when I was unfairly treated by my parents or anyone in authority I learned to shut down, and back away because the consequences to do otherwise would be unacceptable to me. Unfortunately, that became my response with everyone in almost all situations. I was shut down most of the time. Through Project Self-Esteem I discovered the tools for how to effectively stand up for myself in an acceptable way without becoming ineffectual or abusive. I also learned to leave abusive relationships when all else fails.

There was always a lack of communication in my marriage. When the situation became intolerable, and I could no longer hide inside myself, I knew it was time to leave. There was no shouting or uncontrolled acting out when I left. In fact, Carl and I had a better relationship while we lived apart. I had finally learned to stand up for myself.

Before I was born into this world in this life Master, my Oversoul, met with his guides, and they considered what lessons this new person would tackle. They decided self-esteem would play a major role. Therefore, the new life needed strong personalities around it to beat it down, and give it challenges. There were also other karmic lessons set for Master's new life. The new incarnation's parents and husband were not only put together with the new life to work out its karma concerning self-esteem, but also to work out karma on an interpersonal level, karma that was initiated from the interaction of these souls through the centuries in their multiple lives together. Each of the important characters in this new life had other lives with Master's incarnations. These other important people in Master's new life have their own Oversoul, not Master. The other Oversouls would be present at this planning session.

I already mentioned in another chapter that everyone has his or her own energy field called an aura. During our lifetimes the people around us take our energy from us or we take their energy from them. This is done by attacking the other person verbally or physically. Imagine two people facing each other. There is a light, which is actually the person's life force, surrounding him. One person is bullying the other, calling him names, and shoving him. We can see the life force leaving the person being bullied, and going to the bully. The bully is stealing the other person's light. On the other hand, when one person is kind to another person, the giver willingly shares his life force with the other. This giving and receiving of energy creates personal karma.

One of the considerations for the meeting of Oversouls and guides as they plan a new life is to balance out the light that these people took and gave to each other in past shared lives, by allowing them to challenge their issues together.

My mother passed away over twenty years ago. The burden of our shared karma weighed heavily on me. Five years after her passing, I was still deeply grieving, crying uncontrollably for her a few times a week. Nila suggested I go through a soul retrieval process with my mother's spirit to balance our shared karma. I agreed.

At the soul retrieval session, which was facilitated by Nila, who was a certified hypnotherapist, she put me into an altered state. This retrieval happened many years ago so my memories of it are spotty. At the beginning Nila asked me to go back to the first life on Earth I could remember. Suddenly, I was in the body of a big cat, the size of a cougar. It surprised me that I was not in human form. There was the feeling of great danger and pain. My belly was being ripped open by a pack of wolves. I had been hunting to feed my litter of young ones when I was attacked. My babies would be defenseless now, and I was more concerned for their safety than about my own impending death.

Then Nila and I went on to the karma of my mother and myself. I brought forth the tribal life when I was a young man and she was the young woman who bore my child. My mother appeared to me as the young woman. That life and its significance were already familiar to me, and I explained it to Nila. When Nila and I finished discussing that life, the young woman changed form into my mother as I remembered her in my adult years. My mother and I then agreed to balance our karma, and stop the ongoing chain of cause and effect. According to Nila's direction we each gave back with apology the energy we took from the other through our hurtful actions, and received back with forgiveness the life force that the other took. This encompassed all the energy from all the lives we lived together. I saw all the light flowing between us, and felt her pure love without the pain through the centuries of our lives together, even the lives I could not recall. Nila then asked me to release my mother's spirit, and Mom's spirit rose out of my sight.

Immediately, my grief for my mother lessened, and I began to heal. I rarely cry for her now. Instead she is a loving presence with which I can visit when I feel the need. I know that our karma is complete, but we still might meet again in spirit form or have another incarnation together in the future.

Another soul retrieval Nila helped me with was for my karma with my husband. At that time Carl had not yet passed away. We were still acting out our karma, not living together, but seeing each other two or three times a week. Our relationship had improved since we were separated.

The first thing Nila asked me to do once I was in the astral was to go back to the first life in which Carl and I were together. When I felt Carl's energy was with me, I looked to see who we were in that life. Strangely, we were not in human form or any physical form at all. We were pure energy as if we were spirits. I had the sensation of time before any of our material lives. We had been together for eons, since our Oversouls were dim sparks. While our Oversouls help each other to progress, Master's recent earth plane lives have been more spiritually developed, and Carl's Oversoul has been sending down more earth-connected beings. I received this information verbally from my guide Joel who is usually with me on my astral journeys.

Then, in Nila's presence I visited the life of mine in which I was the young woman drawing water from the village well, and was harassed by the young nobleman on his horse. I wondered what the connection was between Carl and I in this life. The answer came immediately. I was shown the baby in the cabin, and told that the woman at the well was the child's mother. She had been repeatedly raped by the nobleman until she became pregnant. Because the child was hers by rape, she found it difficult to love him. My spirit was the mother and Carl's was the child.

My karma with Carl in this life hinges partly on our personal bonds formed in past lives, such as Carl's inability to show affection because I could not love him when I was his mother. Another part of our shared karma deals with my life lessons of self-esteem, and learning to stand up for myself. These are lessons in which Carl is both the obstacle and the learning tool.

Nila and I went through the same clearing process with Carl's spirit as we did with my mother's spirit. Nila instructed Carl and I to return the energy we had taken from each other in this life and past lives, and accept back into ourselves the energy the other person took. This soul retrieval was not as successful as the one I did with my mother's spirit. When I asked my spirit guide Joel why the soul retrieval did not work so well, he told me that my karmic bond with Carl was so complicated and intense that a simple ceremony initiated in the physical world would not be enough to straighten out that web. We two are bonded for all time. Besides that, Joel continued, what made me think that my karma with my mother is complete? The peace I feel with her spirit indicates an improvement of our karmic bond, but we are by no means done with each other. While the soul retrievals helped to restore the balance of some of our energy, there is no such thing as an easy complete fix for karmic bonds.

We have already discussed the karma, which facilitates life lessons, and personal karmic bonds between Oversouls. Two other types of karma are mutable and immutable. Mutable karma is any karma that can be changed by an action of the person. A case of mutable karma might involve a life changing decision such as moving to a new home, marrying someone or dissolving a marriage. There is freedom of choice. In the meeting of

Oversouls and spirit guides during which karmic lessons and working out personal karmic bonds are set up before a spirit comes down to earth, certain life events and possibilities are planned. Due to freedom of choice, and the development, and learning or not learning of life's planned lessons, the karma for the events may change, but the life lessons will stay the same. If we are in a life situation such as a bad marriage in order to learn a lesson, but decide to leave the situation, in this case divorce, without learning the lesson, the same situation will come up again even stronger until we learn what we came to earth to learn. Sometimes we do not learn the lesson. Then we will have the same life lesson in another life.

Immutable karma cannot be changed. Some examples are the era, location, family members, and financial situation we are born into. Our life lessons, physical and personality attributes are also on the list of immutable karma. Certain events and people also cannot be avoided. Life changing accidents, illnesses, and in most cases time of death cannot be changed. In the case of death, suicide is changing karma that should not be changed. It is not planned that way by the Oversoul and spirit guides, and starts a chain of terrible personal karma among the souls who are interacting with the suicide in that life. The uncompleted life lessons of a suicide will have to be repeated in a future life, so nothing is gained by opting out.

Therefore, we see that our karma is set for us by our Oversoul and spirit guides before we come down to earth. We have karma in the form of set life lessons and personal karma which allows us to work out our relationships with other Oversouls. We also have immutable karma, which as a rule cannot be changed, and mutable karma that can be changed due to freedom of choice. Karma is also the law of cause and effect in which we set a string of events in motion by taking an action. Whichever seeds we plant, that fruit is what we will harvest.

CHAPTER SEVEN

OPENING THE CHANNEL

JOURNAL ENTRY
FEBRUARY 12

This was my first trance channeling class at the Learning Light Foundation. I have started taking classes there to discover my hidden psychic gifts and fine-tune the ones of which I was already aware.

Nancy was the instructor. She asked for a volunteer to channel, and I raised my hand. The nine of us in the room were seated around a large oblong table. I rose from my seat, and went to sit in the chair she had set back a little distance from everyone at the table. From across the room Nancy talked me through going into trance. First she instructed me to relax every part of my body one by one, starting from the top of my head. Then we opened my four top chakras, seeing the colors swirl together – green for the heart, blue for the throat, violet for the forehead between the eyes also known as the Third Eye, and the white and gold crown chakra on the top of my head. Then Nancy called in the white light of protection to surround me. I felt the tingling sensation of my soul separating from my body, as though I were going on an astral journey. The concept was like plugging my body into an energy source. In this case, I plugged it into the open channel of energy rising from my crown chakra. Nancy called in any helpful spirit for me. At this time, I had the sensation of another entity's energy sharing my physical body. My body hosted the energy of the other spirit.

My instructor asked me if there were a spirit with me, and if so what was its name. I found it difficult to speak while I was half out of my body. To overcome this, I used the same technique as when I astral travel with Ruth. I run an energy line from the open channel of my crown chakra to my voice box to hum a signal to Ruth. While channeling, I used the same technique to allow the spirit to speak. The guest spirit used my physical apparatus, so while the voice was limited by the physicality of my vocal chords, the tone, speech pattern, and accent were not mine.

In answer to Nancy's question, the spirit gave his name as "Mark". I heard the word, and consciously worked my voice box, yet the voice sounded foreign to me. Through me Mark fielded questions asked by Nancy and the students. We learned from him that he lived in the early 1800's in Spain, and was an aristocrat. I was given the information in words, symbols, and emotions. Although I felt his emotions, I knew they were his not mine, and when I spoke, it was him speaking through me.

Someone at our table asked, "Who is Gabriel?"

I experienced Mark's emotions of being betrayed. Through me he said, "He hurt me."

Another person asked if Mark died when he was eighteen or nineteen years old. Before I felt a response from Mark, someone else asked if he was hurt at age eighteen, and passed away in his early twenties.

I felt Mark's growing anxiety. He had not died at age eighteen, but was badly hurt by Gabriel with a sword wound, and had died in his mid twenties. As he appeared to me he was in his twenties.

At this point, I felt an energy field of someone on the earth plane interfering with my reception from the open channel. It broke my concentration. I told this to Nancy. The feeling was so strong that I disconnected from Mark, and opened my eyes. Nancy, who had moved up close to me, was now backing away. She had moved into my aura to work with my energy field. She asked me to reconnect with Mark, but I could not. He was gone. Other people in the room also knew his energy was no longer there.

A student asked me to describe what Mark looked like. I said he was young, dark-haired, with an olive complexion, and slender. The other person agreed *that he got the same impression, and gave more details of what he saw. I agreed that we were describing the same person.*

I felt very comfortable channeling. This course of classes is where I belong.

FEBRUARY 26

During the channeling classes I have been taking at The Learning Light Foundation, I met my spirit guides Joel and Lilly. Tonight I wanted to introduce Ruth to Joel. Ruth and I sat in chairs in her meditation room. My eyes were shut as I breathed in the white light. My body was relaxed. Concentrating on the area of my heart, I imagined energy glowing from it, becoming bright and hot. I brought in the light to my throat next, working upward through my energy centers.

As I brought the light through my third eye, the quickening started. There was a loud roaring in my ears, and my mind soared to a higher awareness. The roar became more intense when I brought the light through the top of my head. The noise stopped, and I called for Joel's presence. I heard his welcoming voice in my mind, but it took a few seconds for me to make the body connection for speech. His words would come from my mouth, but I would work the muscles. If someone spoke to me while I was channeling, I could hear, but not answer. I could only say Joel's words.

"Joel here. How are ya, darlin'?" He spoke, and the session began.

Ruth asked for her father Stan, and Joel brought his soul into the room. Stan's energy went through me as he sent his love to his daughter. I communicated this to her. I sensed his sadness. When doing medium work like this, I feel the spirit's emotions. Feeling others' emotions is part of being an empath. Stan could hear Ruth, but she could not hear him. Joel acted as a go-between, speaking Stan's words to Ruth.

After Stan left, Ruth asked about her boyfriend Gary. I felt the quickening which was a roaring noise, flashing of lights, and a change of energy. When it settled down, Joel was gone, and I recognized the presence of my guide Lilly. Sometimes she comes to answer questions on relationships. Having evolved to a level six, Lilly's energy vibrates faster than Joel's, and her light is brighter. He is toward the bottom of level five.

In my mind's eye, I see Joel as a large man in his middle years. He has graying hair, and the glint of humor in his eyes. Lilly is ageless, and glows all over. Her hair is golden, and she is dressed in a gown of pristine white.

Lilly gave Ruth advice on her connection with Gary. Afterward, I released my guides with love and gratitude. My own energy flared as their energies left. Picturing the white light draining from my body, I felt it tingle down my feet, and into the floor. The scintillating image of the energy tunneled under the floor, down into the earth like the roots of a tree, and I grounded myself. When my eyes opened, it was like waking up after a long sleep. In fact, I had been under for half an hour.

Ruth was ready to channel, and I guided her into the process, using the method I used for myself. I included a short ritual prayer. It called for divine protection, contact with spirits for her highest good, and no taking of her energy.

She communicated silently with her father, then called in a different soul. I saw the shape and intensity of her aura shift as she channeled a spirit who called herself Rosie. The expression on Ruth's face turned to one of mischief. Her mouth tilted in a half-smile. Laugh wrinkles appeared at the outer edges of her closed eyes. Rosie and I chatted for a while as I tried to discover why she was here. I asked Rosie questions about Ruth. From answers she gave through Ruth, Rosie's message for Ruth was for her to lighten up, and have more fun. After a while, Ruth released Rosie, and came back to her normal consciousness. Ruth remembered the entire session.

Channeling gives me a high-energy buzz, and I feel like a bird flying long after my return. Fear or nervousness are not a part of channeling for me. I learned in a class where the instructor could control our uncomfortable feelings, and I felt safe.

Speaking of my guides, Lilly helped me through a few tough spots years ago, long before I was consciously channeling. At that time, I was a support group leader. I knew the wisdom coming from me was not from my own knowledge or experience. I attributed it to help from above. Now I recognize the energy present during those emergencies came from Lilly. Joel is there for me more on a day-to-day basis when I have a question or problem. His advice is sometimes not what I want to hear, but always for my best good. My guides have become an integral part of my life.

CHANNELING

Channeling means opening our mind to spiritual energy. There are many ways to do this. On a subconscious level there is intuition when we do not recognize the presence of spiritual messages, yet we instinctively know a correct path to take. When we use our talents the process is aided by our spirit guides.

While writing novels, I do not use a formal channeling process. I just keep in mind my objectives for the scene, playing it in my mind as though it were a movie, seeing everything, and feeling like I am a main character in the story. The words that describe what I see in my mind's eye, and eventually are written on paper or go into the computer are a product of my learned art. But I am not in tight control of the characters in the scenes. Every once in a while a scene goes in a direction I do not anticipate. My story writing is a combination of learned art and channeling. I have heard published authors refer to the process as "writing in the zone".

Dreams are sometimes communications from our guides in the spirit world. We dream using symbols much as when we channel. Spirits of those people we are familiar with who have passed away visit us through the energy channel we open during sleep. In dreamtime some people are given premonitions of coming events. The process is sometimes called precognition. Premonitions also happen during waking hours. Our spirit guides open an energy channel from the spirit world into our crown chakra, and give us information.

There are many ways to open a spirtiual channel and receive messages using objects. By objects I mean tarot cards, the palm of your hand, tealeaves, crystal balls, oija boards, etc. Each object is used in a different way to interpret messages from the other side, but there is always energy coming down to bring the message. Therefore, I call it a form of opening a channel.

Some people can read auras, which are people's energy field. The different colors and brightness of the auras figure into the interpretation, as well as intuitive understanding.

The process of opening the channel to the spirit world that I learned in Nancy's class is called trance channeling. The person who channels is in a deep altered state. Not all channels are trance channels. Some readers who use a channel do it while fully aware. I am not one of those people.

While astral travel, like trance channeling, is communicating with the spirit world it differs in a significant way. The initial process of relaxing the body and activating the chakras (energy points on the spine) are the same in both cases. What happens after we rise into the column of light differs. When astral traveling, we reach the doorway to the spirit world, and go through to the other side. A person who is trance channeling stays on this side of the portal, and communicates with spirits. In my mind's eye, my guides come to my side of the doorway. Not all trance channels see a doorway. It is a tool I use to understand the concept. Other people see the channel as a vortex, a whirlwind of energy. In either case, a column of light with a portal or a vortex, the image an astral traveler or channel uses is not important, so long as it works. There is no material portal or vortex. We are talking about our own personal symbol for a change in energy frequencies: the dense, slow energy frequency of the material plane, and the faster, lighter frequency of the spirit plane. Some people do not experience the doorway or vortex at all. How we see the spirit world is open to personal interpretation.

Over the years I have devised a process for trance channeling that is comfortable for me. Some of my clients felt uncomfortable with me allowing my guides to speak through me, using my body, and causing me to sound and appear unlike myself. So I worked out a system of communication with my guides that gives me symbols using visual, auditory, and emotional cues, but does not allow them access to my body. I do the talking myself. I am still in trance, but control of my body is my own. Being an empath, I feel the emotions of people I am reading, even if they are not in the room. Other kinds of information come from my guides.

It does not matter how many people are in the room when I am channeling for someone. I always manage to latch on to the correct person's energy. Once I was doing a group channeling session at a national writers' conference in Dallas. We were in the sitting room of a suite belonging to members of my local California chapter of writers. When I went into trance there were five guests in the room. Each time a different person asked a question she gave me her first name. Joel had no trouble in keeping track of who was speaking, and honing in on the different person's energy. Once or twice I heard the door to the suite open and close, but had no idea if someone was entering or leaving. There were more than five names of people for whom I was reading. When my eyes opened at the end of the session there were ten people in the room beside myself. Joel had been fielding questions from most of them without skipping a beat. I had been in trance for well over an hour, but was aware of what was being said at all times. My focus on the symbols and interpretations was so concentrated that I could not remember most of what went on. A majority of the people were from other chapters thus strangers to me, so the readings could not have been based on my previous knowledge of their life situations. From feedback given to me by some of those who had received a reading, Joel's information was accurate.

I have no fear of evil spirits or evil in general while I am channeling or astral traveling. First, when dealing with the spirit world, I always call in the white light of protection to surround me. Second, my spirit guides are there to protect me, and I trust them implicitly. Only twice in my many years of practicing metaphysics have I been confronted with evil.

Once I was doing a professional reading for someone who wanted me to get rid of a spirit who was annoying her and her family. Joel contacted the spirit, and found that it would attach itself to people, and suck their energy into itself. When Joel initially tried to send it away, it tried to latch onto me, then tried to return to my client. Joel forcefully made it go away. The energy of the spirit seemed to me more mischievous and persistent than evil. There was not much intensity to its power or much presence of dark, heavy energy. Quite a few months later the woman for whom I had channeled told me that the spirit had not returned.

The other instance when I was in the presence of evil was a more intense experience for me. I was doing a group channeling session in the back area of the book and gift shop I owned. It was set up like a living room with a sofa and chairs. There were seven people in the room: myself, my business partner Cynthia, Jane who did the past life regressions in my shop and could visit the spirit world and psychically see what I was channeling, and four lady clients. Usually, only my guide Joel was present at readings, but that night all three of my guides were with me: Joel, Lilly, and Leland. Leland was more of a companion of Master's in the spirit world than a guide for me. The presence of three guides gave me a clue that something unusual was about to happen.

One by one the ladies asked questions, and Joel answered as usual. Then it was Lauren's turn. She asked about the well being of her three month old grandson who had passed away suddenly. The medical community called it crib death, a term used when they did not know the true cause of death when an infant dies in his sleep. That was two years in the past. She wanted to know what was the purpose of its life, and was he all right?

Joel called in the child's spirit to look at its energy. At once, I perceived an evil entity so great that it wiped out my communication lines with all three of my guides. It felt dark, devoid of life-giving light, heavy, and the back of my neck and shoulders tingled in a creepy way. I felt more confused than frightened.

After sitting in the void on the other side for a while, silently calling in my mind for my guides to return, Lilly finally came through. She explained to me that the child's purpose in that life was to save its family by taking on the evil that I saw. It would have destroyed the child's family. A highly evolved soul had volunteered to take the evil entity onto itself by coming down to earth as the child. The evil was attracted to the extraordinary energy, and still possessed the child's spirit on the other side. Lilly, Joel, and Leland were going to do battle with the evil entity to free the child's spirit. As soon as Lilly delivered the message she disappeared again, and I sat in the dark void.

I heard screeching as though an animal were fighting for its life, and explosions of energy like hand grenades going off. All I could think was, this is so bizarre, what could I possibly tell Lauren that she would believe? The truth was too strange. My thinking was that no one at that night's session would believe any of the readings I gave to any one of them because this reading was so unbelievable.

While I was dealing with Lilly and the situation with the child, Jane had been handling the other ladies in the room. She explained to them that I was communicating with my guides, and would be returning to them shortly.

When the din of battle subsided, Lilly returned to me. Through me, using my voice box, she explained to Lauren that the child had been wandering in the spirit world, and needed to be brought to his guides.

She had done this for him. Now he was at peace. I knew that the glossing over of the facts was done because of my concern about the believability issues of the details.

The channeling session continued as though nothing out of the ordinary had happened. At the end, as I was shutting down the channel and grounding myself, I heard Jane speaking to Lauren. She asked whether Lauren understood Lilly's explanation. Lauren said that she did not. Then Jane told her about the evil spirit, the baby's soul taking it on, and dieing to remove it from the physical plane. She also explained about the baby's psychic rescue, which took the form of a battle between my guides and the evil spirit. Lauren asked a few questions for clarification, and seemed to understand the situation. I thanked Jane for helping Lauren. Then I verified for them all that Jane was correct.

As for my experience with the evil spirit, at no time during the channeling did I feel personally threatened. Although I heard my guides battle the evil, I saw none of it, and had no visual impression of the malevolent presence. My guides protected me at all times.

Aside from the subject of evil, this channeling session held unexpected significance for me. I was surprised on two counts: first that Jane was able to "see" everything that went on in my head during the readings, including the events of which I made no mention to the group. She gave credence to my vision of something that most people would doubt. Secondly, Lauren seemed to understand Jane's explanation. I am not certain she believed in the veracity of what Jane said until I gave my corroborating view of the experience, but she was willing to listen, and try to make sense of it. To this day, the session that night was one of my most extraordinary metaphysical experiences.

So we see that channeling means opening our awareness to the spirit world. Sometimes we do it unconsciously, such as using our creative talents, hearing intuitive thoughts or receiving premonitions. More consciously, we can open our channel by using objects or by raising the energy of our chakras. Depending on our natural and developed abilities, we all channel in different ways and to varying degrees.

CHAPTER EIGHT

FLYING WITH THE GUIDES

JOURNAL ENTRY
JULY 24

Ruth and I were on the astral plane in our animal forms, cavorting around my spirit guide Joel. We leaped on him and each other, happy to be Wolf and Panther again. Joel had a grand time acting annoyed, telling us "beasties" to settle down, and quit knocking him about.

Shaman was there too and, after Wolf and I quieted, the four of us flew off together.

We were surrounded by a night sky. The brilliant stars passed us in a blur. Arriving in a dimly lit cave, we were among a multitude of souls. They appeared to me as hazy forms, but their features were distinct. I recognized my parents among them. The crowd of souls was so enormous that it seemed to reach out forever, the vastness of the place not measurable in area, but in light years. I thought this was not the actual total of souls, but a symbol to give us an idea of our tiny part in the immense scheme of creation. I say us plural because Ruth saw the same images. She thought of it as a representation of the spirit world, a sort of introduction.

Leaving the place of souls, Wolf and I followed our guides Shaman and Joel to the campfire on the island we had visited months ago. The Spirit Bird we had seen the last time we were there ascended in the grey veil of smoke floating up from the fire, rising around him in a slow caress. I recognized his huge form and dark feathers. It enfolded Ruth and I to its breast beneath its wings, and rose with us. When we five, Wolf, Panther, Spirit Bird, my guide Joel, and Shaman, were in the sky above the island, Spirit Bird lifted Ruth and I with its wings onto its back, and soared into the night sky. We flew a far distance, sometimes riding on Spirit Bird's back, other times flying beside him flanked by Joel and Shaman. Our speed was so great that stars whizzed past us.

The journey ended at Spirit Bird's home planet, on a ledge overlooking a sun-baked city. Below were buildings of stone, and wide streets crowded with enormous birds that looked like Spirit Bird. The scene was like a biblical movie made in the fifties, with lots of sun, dust, and stone or mud houses. Men were building something with rectangular stones. Each block was many times larger than a man. The men were doing the physical work, but the birds were in charge. As the tremendous stones were hauled across the ground by four-legged, shaggy-furred beasts of burden, clouds of dust billowed up, settling over everything.

Wolf and I wondered what we were supposed to learn here, but the answer was not forthcoming from Spirit Bird or our other guides. We had been journeying for quite a while, and our concentration was quickly waning. I hummed the signal to return to earth.

Our journey was started with nervousness on my part. It had been five months since our last journey together, and I was uncertain we could still have similar experiences, and communicate on the astral planes without either of us speaking. Happily, my fears were proven unfounded. I have taken astral journey and channeling classes, experienced, and witnessed many astounding metaphysical phenomena. Yet, I still have a problem accepting that I am gifted enough to do all that I do. Perhaps, there is no special gift. Maybe, everyone is capable of communicating with the spirit world, but because of fear, disbelief or religious taboos people do not want to explore it or never consider the possibility. That is an idea worth pondering.

SPIRIT GUIDES

I believe spirit guides are any entities from the spirit world that have messages for us. Guides come in many visual forms. Remember that forms we see while channeling or astral traveling are symbols, not physical beings. They are essentially energy. How we choose to see them depends on the cultures we are exposed to, including our religious beliefs. A light being that is interpreted as an angel by a Christian might bring to mind the oriental feminine figure of Quan Yin by a person who was raised in certain sects of Buddhism. Quan Yin is not an angel. There is no equivalent of an angel in Buddhism. Quan Yin is a Chinese symbol for the embodiment of Compassion. Both people encounter the same being, but see a different form. We see universal energy through a cultural screen to make sense of something that is basically formless. Our guides give us the images as a way of communication.

As I explained before, all of us souls strive to advance toward perfection by increasing our intensity of energy. Do you remember my explanation of the evolvement of souls, using the allegory of the seven-lane highway? Less evolved souls travel at a slower speed in the right hand lanes. As we evolve we move to the left into the faster lanes. Spirit guides are souls that help us to evolve. As souls they also strive to evolve. Guiding other souls is their job on the astral planes. Depending on the history of each guide's soul, they may or may not have had lives on the physical plane. Each soul is different.

Oversouls on the astral planes have jobs that help them to advance. Being a guide is a job. There are different kinds of guides. I asked Joel about the guides who help decide a soul's karma before it comes down to earth in a new life. He called in such a guide so I could get my answers firsthand. The fellow looked like a clerk with eyeglasses, and stooped shoulders. He was introduced to me as Barry. Of course this was not a physical person, but a symbol for a middle level office worker. I asked what he did and how he did it?

Barry showed me a flash picture of Master, my oversoul, to represent a soul that was ready to send a part of itself down to the earth plane for a new life. Looking at the comparative energies of Joel, Barry, and Master's auras, I saw there was not much difference. None of them was vastly more evolved than the others. That led me to wonder how a guide that was not superior in evolution to the being he was counseling could steer him correctly? Who made the decisions when it was time to start a new life, and what karmic life goals and challenges were to be faced? What karmic bonds with other souls would come into play?

Since communicating with spirit guides does not require a question to be physically voiced, my thoughts were answered without my words being formed. The clerk had been brought for my instruction so I assumed the images were given to me by him.

The universe sparkling with stars appeared in my mind's eye. Then it filled with pulsating light. This was my symbol for the universal energy, the mother of all creation, and the receptacle of all knowledge and wisdom. A stream of the universal force slowly entered Master until he glowed, and seemed full of light. It reminded me of a ripening fruit. In explanation, the idea was given to me from Barry that when the time was energetically right for a soul to take a large step in evolvement it could decide on a plan, and receive a human body. The universal force makes part of the decision by enhancing the oversoul in preparation, but the oversoul makes the final decision to go through the life process.

It was Barry's job, along with a panel of colleagues, to help map Master's soul's new life. The vision of clerks sitting in front of computers came into my mind. Master's past karmic information was gleaned from the Akashic Record and other sources, and entered into a program for mapping a new life. The computer was just a symbol for the universal force compiling bits of its vast knowledge into a usable form in a file. Master was consulted on various points. When the computer file mapping the life was complete, and the moment was right, a ball of energy separated from Master's aura, and descended into the baby forming in its mother's womb.

By that time, the life guides had already been assigned, as had the future karmic bonds with other souls, and karmic incidents.

But Barry's job was not done.

Since karma must adjust for the soul's freedom of choice, new life paths must be constantly calculated. Based on the original karmic lessons decided upon before birth, the computer program must come up with karmic incidents to suit the new situation.

When I decided to leave my husband after thirty-five years of marriage, my life path changed drastically. The karmic lessons of standing up for myself against oppression, and becoming financially independent were finally realized. Now a whole new set of goals and challenges came into my life. The decision to leave my home necessitated that I find a steady job to support me. I had experience as a bookkeeper in my own bookstore, but had not worked for someone else in that capacity for twenty years. How could I compete in the job market?

I channeled my guide Joel for advice. He told me to create a tri-fold brochure advertisement, highlighting my business expertise with a target toward small businesses. After handing out only three computer-created tri-folds, I had a full-time job. My karmic path was set by my guides and the universal force. Joel merely showed me the way.

So we see that the guides who help set our fate not only chart our course before our birth, but are with us intermittently throughout our life. Another type of guide, what I call a lifetime spirit guide, also supports us from birth to death. My guides Lilly and Joel have already been introduced. They are my lifetime spirit guides. Lilly is a highly evolved soul, about a lane six on the seven-lane energy highway I used as an analogy in Chapter Four. She appears to me as an intense white and gold light. The energy feels feminine, and I communicate with her as I would with a sentient being. I mind-speak to her, and she answers me in words, visible symbols or emotions. I feel safe and comforted in her presence. If I were more clairvoyant, (able to see metaphysical symbols as pictures) Lilly would probably appear to me as an angel. Since my personal belief system places no importance on angels, I see her as pure energy.

The first time I was aware of Lilly's presence I was about forty-two years old. I was facilitating a weight loss support group session of ten people. The members' issues were especially upsetting that day, and emotions were running high. Although I did my best to raise everyone's spirits, the energy in the room evaporated more with each depressing speaker. While I was trained in small group interaction and weight loss counseling, I was not a certified social worker or psychiatric counselor. No one in the room expected me to be one. They just felt comfortable enough with the group to bring up their deeper problems. Nonetheless I was responsible for everyone's emotional wellbeing during those couple of hours. Somehow I managed to lift everyone up enough so she would not leave the room, and head for her nearest source of junk food for a satisfying binge. I also asked for a commitment from the most traumatized members to call other members during the week for support.

The experience was so draining on me that once I was alone in the room I shut the lights off, and closed the door for privacy. Then for a few minutes my body shook uncontrollably with pent up tension. The right words to avoid a disaster had not come from my learned knowledge, training or experience. They had come in symbols and concepts, as though someone were feeding me the knowledge as the need arose. I also felt the energy of another being inside my thoughts. This happened many years before I learned to channel, but I was familiar with metaphysical energy and the spirit world. Years later, when I formally met Lilly in Nancy's advanced channeling class, I recognized her energy from that memorable weight loss group.

Before I knew who my guides were, it was Lilly who protected me while I traveled on the astral planes, and led me to the cottage in the meadow where the old woman and my infant son lived. Her guidance is there for me without my asking.

My lifetime guide Joel is very different from Lilly. His oversoul's energy is about level five, lower or slower than Lilly's. In fact, he is Lilly's protégé. Joel's oversoul has had many lives. One of his lives was as a medieval Irish peddler and adventurer. That is the person he chooses to show me as his image. The first time I met him was during my second of Nancy's channeling classes. He came through me to answer questions for the class, and has been with me ever since. Actually, I recognize his energy from before that time. It is Joel who gives me the images when I write novels. I wrote two novels before knowing he exists. During that first channeling session with Joel he told me he and I were incarnated together before, and will be again. Perhaps that explains the high level of comfort I feel when channeling his energy.

Another type of lifetime guide is the totem. I explained about totems and animal guides in Chapter Two, but there is more to be said on the subject in relationship to other kinds of guides. Totems are guides as seen through a cultural screen. That is to say, while I think I know what totems or animal guides are intellectually, I have not lived in a shamanic culture, and am not familiar with the concept on that level. When I traveled in the shape of Panther on astral journeys with Ruth, I did not consider the animal as my guide. Panther, including its physical and spiritual attributes, was the image I put forth to those beings I met on the astral plane. My affinity for its energy was instinctual, no thought involved. I received no messages or advice from it. Someone born in a shamanic society might receive messages from an animal guide instead of a spirit that appears as an angel. I am reminded of the saying "different strokes for different folks".

One form of animal guide I did have was an entity I call Spirit Bird. It was a temporary guide that came to Ruth and myself while we astral traveled together. Spirit Bird is the guide mentioned in the journal entry at the beginning of this chapter. It took us on a tour of its home planet, but I was unable to understand what it was trying to convey to me, if there was a message at all. Spirit Bird took Wolf and Panther on a few journeys. The more significant ones dealt with an explanation of the universal force, and how to use it. I think of Spirit Bird in terms of a temporary guide in reference to a specific subject rather than an animal guide. Yes, it came to me in animal form, but the essence of bird and its attributes were not the main messages it gave me.

Another animal that came to me during one of my astral journeys was a lion. I am not referring to a lion from the African veldt, but the character from the movie *The Wizard Of Oz*. It was a symbol to me for courage. In this case, the lion was more of a symbol than a guide. My guides are usually not animals or fictional characters.

Now leaving the topic of animal guides, I will go on to the subject of the spirit of a departed loved one. I have been asked many times if that person's deceased spouse, parent, friend or sibling is his spirit guide. Do they come down to help us? Using my definition of a spirit guide: any entities from the spirit world that have messages for us, then yes they can be guides. That is a very broad statement. It does not mean that the spirit of our loved one is constantly looking down on us, ready to give us advice or save us from harm. Some of us have a tendency to attribute a stroke of amazing good luck, like walking unscathed out of a terrible car accident, to the intervention of a dead loved one. Spirits guides do not change our karma. They may be around to support us during such times, but our karma was set by us and our guides before we were born, and our decisions and actions help set them after our birth. Our passed friends and relatives have their own karma to work through. They are not constantly with us. It would be selfish of us to consider a dead family member as a spirit guide, and habitually call him down to help us. We would do better to contact one of our lifetime guides for advice, and leave the souls of our dead loved ones to seek their own advancement.

That brings us to the process of reaching our spirit guides. The technique is the same as channeling any spirit: relax our body, count to six as we go deeper into relaxation, open our top four charkas, fly up through our crown chakra, cover ourselves with the white light of protection, and call in our guide.

I am reminded of the day my guide Joel and I helped Ruth to connect with her lifetime guide Athena. I led Ruth through the steps of channeling until she was at the portal between our sky and the spirit world. She called for one of her guides to come to the door, but she said nothing appeared. In an effort to help her, I opened my chakras, and rose to the portal alongside Ruth. I saw her open channel as a scintillating, golden light going up to the heavens. Joel was with us, and spoke through me so Ruth could hear his instructions. He told her to call in her guide in her mind, while he added his energy to hers. A blond female, all white with huge wings flew to the portal. She reminded me of Lilly, but her energy was different. Ruth had seen her before. Ruth recognized her energy as one she had experienced before as a purple and green light. The guide gave her name as Athena. Joel told Ruth to ask Athena if she would go with us when we travel out-of-body? She said she always was with us, but did not make herself known. From now on she would show herself to help Ruth. Then we all thanked Athena for coming, and released her with love. I expressed my gratitude to Joel, and let him go as well. Ruth and I drained the extra energy down through our body, and into the ground like the roots of a tree.

Now that we know what spirit guides are, and how to reach them, what do we do with them? Before I knew who my guides were or even that I had guides, they were there for me. They were there for me without me calling upon them or praying for help in any way. Lilly gave me the words to calm and inspire the small weight-loss counseling group. She also showed me the way to the cabin in the meadow where I eventually led Ruth. Joel helped me to write novels by running the action like a movie in my mind while I found the words to describe what he showed me. It was only after he answered questions for me during channeling sessions that I recognized his presence when I wrote fiction. He had been helping me write for years before I knew he existed. With the assistance of Nancy and her channeling classes I learned to call in Joel. For many years now Joel appears whenever I channel. There is no need to call him. He is with me even when I do medium work or contact spirits that have nothing to do with him.

When I do channeling sessions for other people or have questions of my own for Joel, I go up to the portal, and speak to him. Joel and my other guides are there to give me truth and advice. When I need help other than advice, I pray to the universal force as a Buddhist does. Guides are not gods or saints granting favors. They are advisors. From guides we get direction so we can take action ourselves. If we seek divine intervention, it is best we call in the universal force in religious or spiritual prayer for what we need. Our guides may help us to that end with advice, but we must gather the power to change. To me, prayer is calling in the universal energy, and aiming it toward a specific purpose.

We have learned in this chapter that spirit guides are entities from the spirit world that have messages for us. There are many kinds of spirit guides, and they do not appear the same to everyone. They are symbols seen through a cultural screen. That means people see spirits that have meaning for them according to their cultural beliefs, including their religion. In conclusion, whether we are aware of our guides or not they have been with us all our life, are with us now, and will be with us for some time after we die.

CHAPTER NINE

SAYING GOOD-BYE FOR NOW

JOURNAL ENTRY
AUGUST 23

Mom visited me today. It has been nearly a year since her passing, and she still on occasion fills me with her presence. I was trimming bushes in the backyard, enjoying the summer heat as it permeated my body. The familiar prickling on the back of my neck and down my arms announced her arrival. I lay the pruning shears on the ground, sat on the grass, and closed my eyes. Her energy surged through me, the excess flowing from my fingertips. Love, hers for me and mine for her, mingled in my heart. Tears misted my eyes.

As time goes on she visits me less often, but the experiences are always intense. Sometimes Mom comes to me at awkward moments, like when I am choosing apples in the supermarket. As the tingling starts I turn my face toward the nearest high display to hide my tears. I know such occurrences are part of the grieving process. But I also know they are connections with her spirit. She is not gone from me. Our relationship has only changed.

I live in the Los Angeles area, and Mom was in Brooklyn. During the week after her funeral I stayed at her co-op apartment. My sister Barbara was there with me. My mother's spirit found me at the funeral home during the service. At that time I had not yet started astral traveling with Ruth, did not know I could do it, and had been doing it for years. But I did know I had certain

75

gifts. In life my mother knew I had metaphysical leanings. In death she must have figured if she could reach anyone, that person would be me.

Mom had been in a nursing home for the previous year due to a severe stroke. So her soul did not find its own way to her Brooklyn apartment. It stayed with her body until the funeral. I did not communicate with her until I was alone in her bedroom, preparing for sleep. A grey fog in a corner of the room was apparent to me, but I was too distraught over the difficult day to consider what it might be. A tingling sensation started at the back of my neck, and spread down my shoulders, through my arms, and down into my fingers. The room did not feel cold to me so I ruled that out, and waited for the feeling to stop. Instead of weakening, it spread and intensified. The experience would have frightened me, except for the feeling of love that accompanied it.

I climbed onto the bed, and sat cross-legged, settling in for whatever came next. My inexperience with medium work left me unsure of what would happen, but I knew enough about the spirit world not to be frightened. I closed my eyes, concentrating on the warm energy and emotion flowing through my body. An image of her came to my mind. She was eighty- five years old at the time of her death, but that night she appeared to be in her late twenties or early thirties, younger than her age when I was born. She had shown me photos of herself when she looked like that.

I felt her anxiety, near panic. "What's happening to me?" Her words sounded in my head, not my ears. Since her stroke the year before, her soul had been in and out of her body, attached to it by the silver energy cord. Now in death there was no silver cord. Her spirit was free-floating. She could no longer settle into her body.

Mom had told me years before that she did not believe in an afterlife. She thought that when a body dies there is no soul to continue. No wonder she was confused when she still had awareness, but no body.

I said, "Look at yourself. You're pure light. You're beautiful."

She looked down at her light body. A smile slowly appeared on her face, grew wider and brighter with amazement. I felt her joy as a physical thing. Much of her communication came to me not verbally, but by me experiencing her emotions. I told her that her body had passed away, and I would help her. But that there were beings in the spirit world better equipped to care for her. A guide was nearby waiting for her to acknowledge him. It was not in the form of anyone I had known in my life, such as a relative. He stepped forward, but she clung to me like a toddler being left with a strange babysitter. Her panic was back. The guide stepped away, but did not leave the vicinity. I knew she would not be alone.

In an effort to soothe her I reassured her she could stay with me for a while. I told her she was free now, not hampered by her sick, inert body. She could go anywhere she wanted with the speed of thought. She could go anywhere in the world exploring, and return to me whenever she wanted. Her excitement washed through me. Soon after her feeling of elation I recognized her desire for me to fly away with her, and the sensation of her trying to draw my spirit up onto her plane. Fear squeezed my heart. Through mind-speak I let her know I could not leave my body consciously. Maybe tonight while asleep I could go with her. She accepted that and flew away.

My awareness of the world returned and my eyes opened. I realized I was smoothing my left thumb over the back of my right hand, just like my mother touched me when I visited her at the hospital and nursing home after her stroke. The gesture was how she let me know she recognized me.

The next night at about 1:30 a.m. as I lie in bed with my eyes closed Mom's spirit came as a blue light to settle on my body. Her energy moved like a mist, slowly swirling, but blackness seemed to be swallowing her light. It was very oppressive and disturbing. I tried to call in the white light. It was an uphill battle. I opened my eyes to loosen the grip of the troubling energy by bringing me back to the material world.

The room was dark, but outlines of the chest of drawers and low dresser were discernible. Taking in information through my physical senses grounded me enough to gain control of myself, and formulate a plan of action. Mom had not known how to protect herself, and inadvertently let a parasitic entity attach itself to her. It had been sucking her energy. She had come to me when I was unprepared and unprotected. Closing my eyes again, I called in the white light to cover the two of us.

The white energy force was very strong. It went through me like flames along my arms, and pulsated heat throughout my body like a furnace. The darkness surrounding my mother disappeared.

I was lying flat on my back on the bed. My arms lifted, forming an arc, and I felt Mom's energy along the inside of the arc as though she were filling the area. It felt like a huge hug. We moved back and forth together in a rocking motion. Her love felt very potent, and I gave her my love in return. After a while I was exhausted and shaking, but she was not ready to stop. Her energy intensified, and the image of her young self came to me. She was vibrant, eager, and happy. My strength was giving out. I could no longer sustain my connection to the spirit world. Yet our ties were so strong that even after I opened my eyes I felt her presence tingling on the inside of my arms.

The next days were busy with close family and guests. In the Orthodox Jewish religion the immediate family of someone who dies sits shiva. That means we sit on low stools and mourn for a week. During that time friends and family come to visit. The front door is left unlocked, and people just walk in. I was constantly surrounded by my brother and sister who sat shiva with me while visitors came in and out. At night when I was finally alone I was too tired to concentrate.

It was not until two nights after Mom's initial contact, around midnight, that I felt her presence again. I called her to me, making the arc with my arms. Her energy filled the arc. I asked her if she was ready for me to call Dad, and have him take her with him. He had passed away thirty-five years before. She answered "yes", with calm acceptance.

In my mind I called my father's spirit to us. His essence came down into the arc with Mom. There was a growing pressure on the inside of my arms, and I had to open the arc to accommodate him. I saw his energy as a white fog as he joined with my mother. He stayed for a short time. Then the pressure in the arc grew lighter. But I still felt my mother's presence. I said, "Mom, why are you still here?" She answered, "Take care of your sister." Then she was gone.

Two weeks later Ruth and I shared our first astral journey. Since then my experience with metaphysics has grown phenomenally. My initial encounters with my mother's spirit would have been vastly different if I knew then what I know now almost a year later. Our interaction would not have been so physical, meaning the energy in the arc of my arms. Also, she would not have had to stay so close to the physical plane to contact me. I would have been comfortable traveling and communicating with her on the astral plane.

Making contact with souls that have passed on to the spirit world is a common occurrence for me now. My ability to reach the astral plane at will has helped me to see how close the living are to those who exist only in spirit. I am comforted by that knowledge.

MEDIUMSHIP

What happens to us after we die?

There are a vast number of versions of what transpires in the afterlife of a human. Each religion has its own idea. Some people do not believe in the existence of a soul at all. Therefore, to them, death of the body means there is nothing when the body is gone. I have experienced too much in the spirit world, corroborated by other people, to believe there is nothing after the death of our body. As to exactly what happens after death I believe people see what they expect to see. The trip through a tunnel with a white light at the far end of it is a popular scenario. In the white light is Jesus or the person's deceased parents or his angel guides, etc. I have also heard of a huge bus station, its vehicles waiting to take us to heaven. And let us not forget St. Peter at the pearly gates.

Since we leave the material world at death, and become beings of energy no longer able to interact on the earth plane as we did during life, physical forms we see on the astral planes are only symbols. They have no substance. We interpret what we experience according to what we believe. We still rely on our five physical senses to make logic of our surroundings, although our physical sensory organs no longer function. The figure coming to greet us in the nimbus of white light is only energy, and might be identified as someone or something else by another person.

Those who do not believe in an afterlife are confused at the time of their death. Since they still have awareness while the body is not functioning, they think that somehow they are still alive. My husband passed away eight years ago. He was a consummate scientist. If science could not yet explain a concept, then the concept was erroneous. He had fallen, hitting his head on the corner of his nightstand, causing internal bleeding. He was on blood thinners. By the time he was found his brain was destroyed. We took him off life support and he survived, relying on his own physical resources for four days.

Since his physical body was so devastated I rose to the spirit world to speak with him. Most of the time I did it while home alone, not in the hospital with his body. He was under a heavy morphine dosage as well as severely brain-damaged. Our contact would have been on the soul level in any case. The first time I channeled Carl his astral body appeared grey,

79

very dense, and cemented to his physical body, sort of asleep. Although I tried to engage him, he showed no response. A day later I tried again. This time his astral body was bright yellow. I recognized the light of his parents off to the side. Carl thought he was only dreaming. He saw his parents who he knew were dead, and me who he knew was alive. To his mind the dead could not exist in the same place as the living, therefore he must be dreaming. In a sense he was right. People astral travel in their sleep during dreamtime, and his body was in a coma, aided by morphine. In this case, his dream was a real communication with his parents and me. I spoke with Frances and Murray, Carl's parents, and they told me they would help ease his passing. Indeed, every time I channeled Carl during his transition they were present.

Dealing with Carl in the astral after his death was a unique experience. His own physical body was uncomfortable and unresponsive, or non-existent after it was cremated, and he frequently tried to ground his spiritual self through my healthy body. When souls of the dead seek contact with me, usually it is a communication of my energy with theirs in mind-speak. It is a gentle interchange respectful of my boundaries. Carl's communication was more like an invasion. Within seconds of me rising to the astral plane I felt his energy shoot into my body from the top of my head down through my feet, and into the ground. My thought was he was more interested in experiencing the material world again than he was in conversing with me. For weeks when we did communicate, the subject was usually our son. The topic of death was off limits. He would not acknowledge his parents who patiently waited nearby. He refused to give up his belief that a part of himself could exist without his body. Even in death he did not give up his certainty in pure science. He hovered over the familiar material world, waiting to disappear into nothingness.

So we see that our belief system during life has a strong affect on what we think happens at our time of death. While we are on the subject of souls making the death transition this is a convenient time to discuss ghosts. Those Halloween costumes that look like a white sheet draped over a person's head are not far from the truth. On a dark night a ghost would look like fog skimming along the ground. Remember at the beginning of this chapter my description of the grey fog that was my mother's spirit in the corner of her bedroom. Her soul was still earthbound, meaning she had not yet gone up into the light. Ghosts are deceased people whose soul has not made the transition from matters of their material life to rejoin with their oversoul. They hover in the dense atmosphere of the earth plane, watching what is happening in their old familiar surroundings, sometimes trying to communicate with the living. The concept of transparent ghosts flying around a cemetery is deceiving. Material objects hold energy from people who touch them. The more contact between them the more energy is retained by the object. Likewise, dead bodies hold the energy of the soul that inhabited them. When people go to cemeteries to visit their dead loved ones they might feel the deceased's energy present. That energy is not necessarily a ghost. The residual energy in the body has no consciousness. It does not hear or see us. There might be ghosts present, but more likely we would encounter the returning spirit of the person we came to visit. By "returning" I mean it has already gone to join its oversoul on the higher astral planes. The spirit has gone on, and is evolving. It returns to the cemetery because we are calling it down by the force of our intention. We are telegraphing our openness to making contact with it. Earthbound ghosts do not have the same gleaming light as spirits that have gone on.

Ghosts can be helped to refocus their attention from the physical world, and go up into the light. The process is called psychic rescue. When Carl refused to make the transition I felt helpless. Usually, when I contact a spirit unable to cross over I can call in a guide to lead the way. Carl was not ready to leave. A couple of months passed since his death, and he was still lingering around the earth plane, grounding through me. Every time we made verbal contact, I tried to help him cross over. Every time he refused. One evening when I visited with him one of his guides was present. It took the form of an old man in a long gown. Carl was ignoring him. I acknowledged the guide with a nod. Thoughts floated through my mind that I knew were not mine. The guide nodded, and I knew these ideas came from him. He told me to take Carl to the place of his ancestors. In shamanism there is a place on the astral planes where the souls of each family congregate. I do not necessarily believe in the concept, but the guide did not ask me to believe. He was only trying to convey the concept of a family gathering of passed souls. During this time Carl was unaware that his guide and I were conversing in mind-speak.

"Come with me," I told my husband, holding out my ethereal hand. "Let's fly out into the universe together."

Carl held back. His fear that I would take him to the place of death emanated from his energy field. He shook his head no.

"I am alive. I have to come back to earth," I said. "So long as your energy is connected to mine you will come back." Again I extended my hand.

He hesitated then clasped it. Together we flew through the night sky. Eventually, we came to a place lit up like daytime. It was a field crowded with people. Three men separated themselves from the group, and came up to us. I felt great joy and relief rise up in Carl's energy. Two of the men were familiar to me. One was his uncle Paul, the other his cousin Noel. Both had passed away. The third I assumed to be his uncle Mac, Noel's father who had died before Carl and I had met. They hugged Carl, mingling their energy with his. Carl's face was glowing. He was laughing with his relatives, all trace of fear gone. I stepped back and away from them to give them room. Murray and Frances stood to the side, wearing smiles.

Carl's guide said to me, "Let go of his hand."

In the material world I would have been standing too far from Carl to be holding his hand, but on the astral planes this was only a symbol for our energies being connected. I was being told to release my hold on my husband.

"But I promised to take him back with me," I said, thinking my departure would be a terrible betrayal.

"Look at him. He will not miss you. He belongs with us now."

Carl was leaving with his uncles and cousin, his parents trailing behind. He did not look back for me. I saw the wisdom in the guide's words, and let go of Carl's hand. Soon all traces of his energy were too far away for me to see. I knew he had crossed over. My solo journey back to my body was brief, but fraught with emotion. Carl was truly gone. He was free to continue his evolution.

Since that time we have met on the astral planes. He thanked me for helping him leave the earth plane. There were no hard feelings toward me for the way it was done. He told me the decision was not mine, but belonged to his guides and oversoul. From his explanation I realized that psychic rescues are not metaphysically talented people interfering with the karma of stuck souls. The situation is more like guides and oversouls using these intermediaries for their own purposes. I have no issue with that. It takes responsibility for that action off my shoulders.

I asked my husband what it felt like going to the other side. He said, "The veil dropped from my eyes, and I could see everything in heaven and on earth. I could see forever. Memories of my life on Earth paled in significance."

Which brings us to what happens to the soul after it passes from the vicinity of the physical plane. According to metaphysics a soul undergoes a period of debriefing. During this time the oversoul, with the aid of its guides, gleans the karmic lessons it has learned in that life. It also looks at the advancement in energy it has undergone. The soul that lived on earth again becomes a part of the oversoul, with a bit of its energy going to the Akashic Record. That small bit of energy is not lost forever to the oversoul. Like blood in the human body, it is replaced. Learning karmic lessons and gaining wisdom enhances the oversoul's energy. Also the prayers of people on earth for the dead add energy to the corresponding oversouls. Each of an oversoul's lives becomes part of its memories. When someone on earth calls for the help or presence of a departed spirit, the oversoul allows that part of its energy to fly down to earth for a while. The soul visits with the human then returns to the oversoul.

Calling down the spirits is called mediumship or medium work. A person who does this is called a medium. The process of calling in the dead differs from one medium to another, and sometimes a medium can do it in more than one way. When a soul decides to visit someone on Earth without waiting for an invitation I call it a spontaneous event. There is no intent for communication by the living person. A tingling on the back of the neck or in the fingertips accompanied by a thought of someone who has passed away is a sign of a spirit's desire for contact. We all get signals from the spirit world. Not all of us know what it is or care to acknowledge it. In order to receive contact all that is needed is for us to close our eyes, and allow the spirit access.

If we seek contact with someone who has passed, the process is the same as channeling. In fact medium work is simply opening a channel into the spirit world. The only difference is we are calling to a specific spirit that has known us during its life or knows the person on whose behalf we are channeling. As part of a normal channeling session a client might ask me to bring in a dead friend or family member, and I would send out energy toward that being. That is not the same for me as when I plan a medium session for someone.

The way I do a planned medium session is different from how I have seen other mediums do it. Instead of me calling in the soul, and interpreting everything for the client I prefer to bring my client up to the spirit world with me, helping him to contact his loved-one personally. The process is started with hypnosis to bring the client to the portal on the astral planes. Then I ascend and call in the spirit. We remain on our side of the portal the entire time. I hold the client's hands so we share the energy, creating a circuit. When the spirit joins us its energy melds with the circuit. The client asks questions of the spirit directly, not through me. I help with the interpretation of the symbols, seeing what the client sees.

After my sister Barbara passed away my brother Marty and I were sitting shiva for her at his home. He asked me to channel Barbara for him. I agreed, but with one stipulation, that he come with me to the portal to see her. Although Marty is spiritual, practicing the Orthodox Jewish faith, he is also an accountant, very grounded in the material world. Neither of us was certain he could reach Barbara, but he was willing to give it a try.

We sat opposite each other on our low stools. Following my instructions, Marty closed his eyes, and relaxed. Since he was new to channeling I led him through the entire hypnosis process, starting with relaxing every part of his body from his head down. Next we opened his top four chakras, and he ascended to the portal. He waited there for a few seconds while I took the fast track up, descending six steps down into relaxation, opening my chakras to the count of four, and rising to the doorway. Marty twitched as I took hold of his hands. I called in the white light of protection to surround us, and saw the scintillating energy descend to cover us.

At our invitation Barbara came to the portal. I was surprised at her bright light. In life she was racked with mental illness. Her personal energy was dark, and she sucked the light from other people. In death her light was brilliant, like that of my guide Lilly.

Marty said, "Is that Barbe? She's so bright." He sounded uncertain.

"Yes. It's her," I answered. "People look different on the other side.

Often the most evolved souls take on the hardest lives. Meeting difficult challenges helps souls evolve faster."

I felt the warmth of Barbara's love pump into my heart, through my body, into my hands, and out to Marty.

"What do you feel in your hands?" I asked my brother.

"Heat. It's very hot. Where is it coming from?"

"It's coming from Barbe. She sends her love. Sit in the energy for a minute, and feel it go through you. In your mind send her your love."

We three melded with the loving energy that raced through the circuit.

"Ask her what she thought of the funeral." Marty said.

Although Barbara was Catholic she was buried in the Jewish cemetery where our parents are buried in the family plot. Marty had gone through considerable effort and expense to arrange for the rabbi, the funeral parlor service with many of our relatives attending, and a meal for everyone in a restaurant after the burial.

A symbol from my sister flashed through my mind's eye. It was a picture of her casket being lowered into the grave.

"Tell me what you see," I said.

"I see her casket, but I don't understand. What is she telling me?" He asked.

"I also see the casket," I replied. "It's going down into the ground." Words sounded in my head, and I repeated them. "She says you lay her body to rest with her family, and she thanks you for that."

"Yes. I see it going down into the ground, but what about the funeral? What did she think of it?"

Again she showed me the box going into the grave, yet there was an incomplete feeling coming from Barbara. She was not at rest.

"Marty, she was Catholic. Barbe is waiting for the Christian funeral at the church. She hadn't seen any of the people at the Jewish funeral home in over eighteen years. The only thing she cared about that day was being put in the cemetery with Mom and Dad."

There was silence for a few moments while he digested what I said.

"I see," he finally nodded. "She's okay with being in the Jewish cemetery, but she's waiting for Wednesday's funeral at the church."

"Yes." I felt relieved that he understood.

Together the three of us sat in our combined energies, basking in each other's love until Barbara separated her presence from the circuit. Marty and I thanked her for being with us. Then I helped Marty make the transition from the portal to earth.

"See Barbe's light go through the doorway," I said. "It gets smaller and smaller as it recedes until she disappears," I guided him. "Now imagine a trap door shutting down over your crown chakra, the white-gold light coming from the top of your head. The light is gone. Next shut the door down on the purple light between your eyes. See it disappear. Shut down the blue light, and the green light. Picture your extra energy, moving down through your body, starting from the top of your head, into your feet, and into the floor. It passes into the ground like the roots of a tree."

I then counted backward from six, instructing Marty to wiggle his fingers and toes before opening his eyes. Once he was back on the earth plane, I grounded myself in a similar way, but much faster.

Marty told me his channeling experience was enlightening. He wanted to know if our sister was all right. In life she was very troubled and angry. He was surprised and happy to see her energy so bright. Her light is what he hoped to see, but did not expect. As far as being nervous about channeling for the first time, Marty believed in my talent. I had done psychic readings for him for years with good results. He was not uneasy at all.

The reason I suggest clients make personal contact with their relatives' and friends' spirits is the experience seems more real to them. When they see the symbols, and feel the love they are more likely to believe there was true contact.

Many people do not want to channel. They prefer I contact the dead. I understand. Death can be a scary prospect. For many people it is the great unknown filled with the possibility of hell, the devil, ghosts, zombies, vampires, and other monsters. When it comes to religious beliefs like God, heaven, hell, the devil, and angels I will not say that anyone is wrong. Some of it is just not in my experience. According to the metaphysical explanation there are seven planes of energy called the astral planes. The slower vibrating planes have less energy. Less evolved souls reside on the planes with less energy. If you think of the seven planes vertically with those of higher energy on the top and those of lower or less evolved energy on the bottom, the concept of the most beautiful light or heaven is above, and the least light and least evolved spirits, those with negative or dark energy are down in hell. I personally do not believe in the concepts of heaven and hell. Those are biblical terms. As a Buddhist I do not believe in The Bible. As a metaphysician I do believe in the astral planes. Some people who believe in metaphysics also believe in Christianity or other religions.

Death is explained in different ways by different religions. Which brings us full circle to where this explanation of death started. There are a couple of points I would like to make before this chapter concludes.

First, people have asked me to channel their children who have passed on. In the karmic scheme of things the souls of dead children are not highly invested in their life. The length and scope of the karmic plan for that short of a life is not very complicated. The bonds with other people have not had time to grow and develop. In contrast with other lives of an oversoul the life that is cut short in childhood is not very karmically significant. It is the karma of the child to die young, return to the oversoul, and to return to the physical plane in another life. The karma of the family suffers the loss, and deals with the loss. In most cases the family suffers more than the child.

The last point is about zombies, vampires, and ghosts. Zombies and vampires are fiction. They are solely the products of literature about reanimated dead bodies. Ghosts on the other hand are a metaphysical reality. They are disembodied souls. There have been a multitude of stories about ghosts both published in print, and in the oral tradition. Most of what has been written in stories and told over campfires is a figment of the author's imagination, but the phenomena of ghosts are a reality. Mediums cannot reach beings like vampires and zombies because they do not exist, but we can contact the souls of people who have died, because disembodied souls are real.

Medium work can be very rewarding, helping us to make sense of life and death. It also helps us to continue our relationship with relatives and others who have passed on, and to understand what happens to us after we die.

CHAPTER TEN

SHOWERS OF ENERGY

JOURNAL ENTRY
MARCH 31

We had returned, Ruth and I, to the nighttime campfire meeting of souls. Flames leaped and danced from the burning wood within the ring of stones, throwing light and shadows across the faces and forms of the gathered celestial citizens. Joel and Shaman were with us on this journey. Spirit Bird soon came forward and beckoned us to fly with him.

The five of us, Ruth and I in our human forms, our two guides, and Spirit Bird flew to the planet of the birds where we had been on our last journey. I recognized the arid landscape and stone buildings as we came in low and landed. A magnificent edifice stood before us. It was made of huge blocks of what looked like dark marble. As we entered I felt the holiness of the place. I knew it was a temple although I saw no altars or figures to worship. Toward the center of the huge temple lit by torches on the dark marble walls a lone figure stood waiting for us. It was a massive black bird that reminded me of a carved totem. His power was so intense that it frightened me, but Joel put his arms around both Ruth and I, letting us know everything was all right. Spirit Bird introduced us to Black Bird, He was the guardian of the temple.

Black Bird led us to a corner at the back of the temple. A great gush of air and energy, spouting like fireworks came up through a hole in the floor. The geyser was over twice my height. The thought came to me that the energy fountain emerged straight up from hell. Ruth and I were apprehensive, clutching each other's hand, but our guides calmed us, letting us know they were near, and there was nothing to fear. Then souls flew up amid the fiery sparks. They were transparent amorphous beings, but recognizable in flashes of facial features. Ruth's ex-husband Bill was first. Then came my mother and father and Ruth's father. There were also many other souls, but none either of us recognized.

I do not remember moving into the energy stream, but suddenly Ruth and I were in the geyser, clinging to one another among the souls, letting the power surround and lift us. I felt glorious, the tingling heat energizing me physically, and rocketing my emotions skyward, feeling at one with all the spirits present, and throughout the universe.

When the two of us had rejoined our guides outside the column of power I asked what this world was, and what the birds did here.

Spirit Bird answered, "This place is on a plane much higher than the plane the planet Earth is on. The birds work with energy."

The concept of working with energy intrigued me, and I wanted to know more, but I experienced discomfort coming from Ruth. I did not know if it was the dark temple, Black Bird or the souls in the column of power disturbing her. But I heard her projecting, "Let's get out of here."

Accepting Ruth's instincts, we left the temple and planet of the birds. Our guides Joel and Shaman went with us, but Spirit Bird remained on his world. Ruth and I morphed into Wolf and Panther. We flew to the wolf place where we were comfortable.

I asked Joel the purpose of tonight's journey. He said it was to show us the power of the universe, and that it was at our disposal. We have to learn to use it. At the same time Ruth asked the same question of Shaman, and was given the same answer. Then Ruth and I felt the universal force showering around us. The sky was filled with it, and we took off, flying through the energy, glorying in it. Eventually we saw the planet Earth below us, and knew it was time to go home. I toned the signal to return to the physical plane.

Ruth's experience was closer to mine than usual. She remembers briefly going to the campfire where Spirit Bird met us, and guided us to his realm. She also saw Black Bird in the temple, and the spirits rising in the undulating light that shot up from the floor like a geyser. The same spirits of family members that I saw were recognizable to her. She remembers standing in the column of energy with me, soaking it in as I did. Her discomfort that I clued into was her feeling that we did not belong in the same energy with the dead souls. It was too soon. At the end of the journey she asked Shaman about the message she should take with her from tonight's journey. His answer was, "Power. Take the power and use it." Ruth said the universe was on fire. At the very end she recalls the two of us hugging in the astral with the warmth and light around us.

JOURNAL ENTRY
JULY 15

(This is an account of a journey of mine with Nila five years after my last flight with Ruth.)

Nila and I were again astral traveling while we sat on the patio of my home. We were opposite each other in chairs, holding each other's hands.

I remember following running horses, flying after them. That is a symbol of mine for astral traveling through the dimensions. Soon we came to a nighttime campground with many fires across the land. Beings from different galaxies sat around the fires. The creatures were in many forms, some with more than four limbs, others with more than two eyes, one eye or none at all. There were scaled bodies, furred or feathered ones, and many other textured skins and protective coverings, in all colors of the rainbow. Nila saw the campfires and strange beings as well. We also saw the two tall black-robed men we had seen in a previous journey together.

As happens in dreams and astral journeys we suddenly found ourselves in a different place. I was at the top of a high steep mountain in the shape of a witch's hat. Power encompassed me, tingling and warm throughout my body. It poured into my head, and out through my hands. I felt like a sorcerer, ruling the universe. The power was so overwhelming that I decided to ground myself by returning to one of the campfires, and giving the energy to one of the extraterrestrial beings. Maybe the being would be better equipped to handle it. But the power would not leave me. I went back to the top of the mountain where the energy flow petered out after a few minutes.

Nila also saw the two black-robed men, and the campfires with otherworldly beings sitting around them. She too saw a similar shape to the mountain I stood atop, a huge stone pyramid. Nila went inside the pyramid, *and experienced what she called The Milky Way power, the power of our galaxy. It was terrifically strong, and she had trouble grounding herself so she could control it. Nila told me when she has difficulty grounding she visualizes herself being flushed down a toilet to send the energy into the earth, but this time even that method did not work. She had to wait until the power dissipated at its own pace.*

After the power left us we grounded ourselves with our usual visualizations, and returned to the physical plane. I had never before felt such an intense energy flow. Nila was also impressed with the experience.

When Nila and I astral travel together my expectations for the journey are different from when Ruth and I flew in tandem. In all cases I see symbols, but the energy feels different when I am with a different partner. I am in awe of Nila's metaphysical knowledge and abilities. When we are in flight we visit locations unlike the kind of places Ruth and I visited. The energy is more intense with Nila. The campfires of the beings from throughout the universe that I saw with Nila were counted in the thousands, spread across square miles of hills. My campfire experience with Ruth was only one fire on a tiny island, and consisted of a small gathering of otherworldly beings. While the shower of power in the temple of the Birds was glorious, it was a small fraction of the power that streamed through me on the mountaintop while I traveled with Nila. I suspect the intensity of my astral journeys varies depending on the power of the combined energies of the partner with whom I am traveling and me.

METAPHYSICAL ENERGY

Metaphysical energy, also known as the white light by psychics or prahna by yoga practitioners, God's love by monotheists or Buddha nature by Buddihists is the universal force in all things on every plane of existence. It is not magic, but scientific, as real as electricity or atomic power. The scientific community is just not able to explain it yet.

The way the difference between the material plane and the higher astral planes was explained to me was the energy on higher planes vibrates at a faster speed than the energy in the material world. Everything in the universe has this energy, including people, spirits, furniture, and even rocks.

The psychic energy force in people is centered in our chakras. Chakras are energy points on our spine. Depending on the culture offering the information, there are between seven to twelve chakras. I prefer the simpler seven chakras path. This starts with our red colored root chakra at the base of our spine, also called the kundalini. It is in the area of our anus and intestines, and has the lowest speed of vibration. Our survival instincts are located there. Next chakra up is orange, and is in the area of our belly just above our genitals. Regeneration is its function, including sexual energy, and creation. Our intuition or "gut feel" comes from our third chakra up the spine. Its color is yellow, and it resides in the area of our stomach. Next on our spine is our heart chakra. It is green, and is where our heart is seated. Our heart chakra is known as our center of emotion. Above our heart chakra is our blue throat power point. This is the place where our communication skills are empowered. Rising to our next chakra to a place on our forehead between our eyebrows is what we call the third eye. It is violet. We call it the third eye because it is the area through which we experience or "see" the metaphysical world. Above our violet power point is the crown chakra on top of our head. I see it as a gold or white light that connects us to the spirit world. You may remember when we channel or astral travel we ascend through the light of our crown chakra to get to the door of the spirit world.

When we open the power of our top four chakras, the speed of our vibrations accelerates, and we reach the higher astral planes. Our bottom three chakras are earthbound, keeping us grounded in the physical world. The upper four are sky-bound, and help us ascend.

The colors of our chakras permeate our body, and create a colorful power display around us called our aura. Some of us vibrate on a level that permits us to see people's aura. If I concentrate on a person in a certain light I can see that person's energy field, but not in color. To me it looks like white or golden light. In paintings of Jesus Christ or saints many times the artists have painted a white or golden light around the subjects' head. In common terms we would call it a halo. Actually, it is the bright crown chakra of a psychically powerful person.

About twelve years ago I was at a psychic fair, and had a color photograph taken of my aura. The camera was hooked up to a computer, but did not look unusual. I did not expect much, but was pleasantly surprised. What I received was two photos, and a fourteen-page printout of the meaning of the photos. Basically, the pictures showed my light as bright green with an outer border of yellow. At first I was disappointed that my aura was not violet, the color of the third eye chakra. To my way of thinking at that time the higher the vibration of the color of my aura the more psychically open I would be. Then, thinking of who I am, it was obvious to me that green had to be the basic color of my aura. I am an empath, experiencing my world through my emotions, reading other people by feeling their emotions. The heart chakra, which is the origin of our emotions, is green. Half of my wardrobe was green, and my new apartment was furnished in green before I knew the color of my aura. Green is the color of my life.

Psychic energy is as physical as other kinds of energy that scientists recognize. In fact I experienced two instances when my psychic energy interfered with energies known by scientists. A friend of mine asked me to do a channeling session for her on the telephone. As my chakras opened and vibrated faster I heard a buzz on the phone line. The more chakras I opened the louder the noise was on the phone. By the time I flew up through my crown chakra the noise was like three police car sirens going on at once. It gave me a headache, and I told my friend I could not do a reading under those circumstances. I had to shut down my chakras. She also heard the noise on the line, and agreed that we should not continue. As the energy left my power points the noise on the phone line subsided. When I was fully grounded the phone line was quiet again. There was something about the frequency of my aura while I was channeling that interfered with the energy frequency of that particular telephone line.

On the same subject of psychic energy, other incidents occurred during my channeling sessions held after closing hours at a retail shop I owned. Occasionally, my business partner Cynthia and I shut the window blinds, and conducted group-channeling readings. I was the channel. One night after a channeling session we opened the blinds and saw a police car outside in front of the jewelry store next door. The shop specialized in custom jewelry made with diamonds and gold. When we asked what happened the owner told us that in order to protect their inventory they had an elaborate burglar alarm. Their sophisticated system included a sensitive light trigger that was silent, but notified the police department when there was a light disturbance. Tonight's incident seemed to be a false alarm, but he wanted to know if we heard anything unusual or if anything unusual happened with our electricity. No, none of us in the shop had heard anything unusual and our lights were off. We had used candles for the little light we needed. My neighbor was upset because there had been a few false alarms lately, and they could not figure out why. The one thing they had noticed was that each time the false alarm went on our window blinds were closed, but we seemed to be inside the store. This false alarm problem had never happened before our shop opened. He was convinced we were doing something to set off his alarm. I knew psychic energy could affect other types of energy, including electricity, infrared, and ultra-violet light, but did not mention it at the time. The police in our city were not fans of psychic practitioners, and I did not want to draw attention to myself.

That was not the only instance my psychic abilities were related to a burglar alarm misfiring. I was sleeping at my cousin Sandy's home. They did not set their alarm because they thought I might accidentally set it off by opening a window or door. At about two a.m. I was awakened by a shrill noise. It was so annoying that I put my hands over my ears to shut it out. I heard my cousin and her husband talking in the hallway. They were trying to turn off the alarm, but nothing worked because they had not set it in the first place. Sandy called the alarm company, but they could not help.

Sandy knew I had received a second-degree Reiki certification and energy adjustment a few days before, and suspected my energy enhancement had set off her alarm. The noise went on for a half hour. Nothing she or her husband tried turned it off. She asked me to try shutting it down by channeling. In case my energy had caused it, maybe I could do something to stop it. I agreed to try.

Alone in the bedroom I sat on the bed, closed my eyes, and opened my top four chakras. Then I called the energy in the house to enter my body, and go through me into the ground. The heat of the energy tingled inside me as it entered my head, and worked its way down through my feet, and into the ground. I do not know how long I was in the trance, but it was longer than a few minutes, and shorter than thirty minutes. The alarm was still raging as I shut down my chakras, and closed the channel. Within two or three minutes the alarm cut dead. The next morning I asked Sandy what they had done to turn off the alarm. She said they had not done anything. It just quit. Their alarm system never malfunctioned like that again. Neither Sandy nor the alarm company discovered a scientific reason for the incident.

Since I mentioned Reiki this would be a natural place to discuss healing energy and healing touch. Reiki is a form of energy healing that originated in Japan. It incorporates chanting specific mantras with channeling the universal force through the practitioner, and transferring it to the patient. The healing energy helps bring the body's energy into harmony.

Reiki is one of many kinds of energy healing techniques that can be taught, while some people are simply born with the ability to heal. I do not profess to be a healer of any kind, yet I have had myself healed with psychic energy.

One evening I took part in a spirit circle at The Learning Light Foundation. There were over twenty people participating. The leader enclosed the circle in an opening ceremony, calling in the protective spirits of the four directions. She then guided us into the spirit world by opening the chakras. The facilitator then called in spirits. I felt the presence of disembodied souls. Their energy caused a prickling sensation on the back of my neck, but no messages came through them for me. There was no dramatic connection made with any of the other channels, and I was disappointed until at the end of the session we were told by the leader to bring the healing energy of the universe into the circle. The energy combined the collective resources of the open channels of all the participants in the circle plus that of the visiting spirits. We each sent the energy to people we knew outside the circle in need of healing. Then we were told to lay our hands on a part of our own body that needed healing.

Ten months before I had over-reached sideways to pick something up from the floor, injuring my right shoulder. I had not had it treated, and still had a lot of pain. There was little range of motion, and I could hardly lift anything. With my eyes closed I pictured the scintillating universal energy flow down into me through my open crown chakra, permeate my body on its way to my hands, and out through my fingers, into my shoulder. The energy also found its way to my shoulder through other paths in my body. Immediately after, the circle was brought to an end.

To my amazement my shoulder felt much better. As I drove home I tested my shoulder, finding much of the pain gone, and much more mobility than I had regained in the past ten months combined. Over the next four days my shoulder continued to heal until it was well again. Until that spirit circle energy healing was only a theory I hoped was true, but had my doubts about. Now I do not doubt it. Does it work every time? I do not think so or know why it does not. But I do know that occasionally it does happen.

As mentioned before, Reiki healing uses the power of chanting to enhance the energy flow. Chanting is also used in prayer in many religions. As a Nicheren Buddhist I chant a mantra. Reciting the mantra lifts my vibrations up so my spirit rises out of my body without the ritual of opening my top four chakras. Chanting causes sound vibrations, and the intent of the prayer is a focus for energy. My theory is the combination of sound vibrations and energy from my human aura lifts my spirit to the frequency of vibration of the higher astral planes. Not all people who chant are elevated out of their body. This is a proposed explanation of why it happens to me.

Although my spirit leaves my body while chanting the Buddhist mantra, I do not make contact with my guides or go through the portal at that time. When I pray I experience energy coming into my crown chakra from the universe. My prayer infuses the desired direction for the energy, and sends it out through my hands back into the universe. I use prayer to seek help, and spiritual guidance. Channeling sessions with my guides are for answering questions for other people, medium work, and astral journeys. I do not combine or confuse prayer with astral travel.

Not only do people have their own aura, they leave bits of their energy behind on the objects they touch. Jewelry worn every day such as a wedding ring retains its owner's auric prints to an astonishing degree. Some psychic readers have the ability to hold someone's ring, and see his past, present and future. This is called psychometry.

Historical museums and antique shops are unique experiences for me. When I was twelve years old I was in the Brooklyn Museum, walking through a colonial American exhibit. The display held artifacts of a family room of a small cottage set up with original seventeenth or eighteenth century kitchen utensils: a kettle hanging in the fireplace, clothing hung up on a wall, pewter place settings on the trestle table, etc. There was only a rope guard, no glass separating the antiques from the visitors, nothing to shield the energy from the historical objects from me. The antiques were of a sort to be used every day by the same people. They were rich with the energy of the family that used them. The display was set up against a wall in a short passageway so there was a wall just behind me also. The energy in the space had nowhere to spread out, and was concentrated. I felt abject sadness surrounding me, as of someone in mourning for not only people lost, but hope destroyed. Colonial life was hard. I knew the emotion was not mine, but belonged to the owner of one of the utensils, perhaps more than one utensil or person. My parents had taught me there is no such thing as spirits, ghosts, and the occult in general. I did not understand what was happening to me, and ran out of the room crying. Years later with knowledge of my psychic gifts I understood my reaction to the energy in the display was linked to my empathic nature. I interpreted the personal energy held by the artifacts through my emotions.

Antique shops are also psychically charged for me. I only go into one to accompany a friend, never for my own curiosity or gratification. Before entering an antique shop I close off my chakras from outside energy and drain my psychic energy into the ground. That lessens the effect of the auric energy coming from the objects in the shop. I also try not to touch anything.

Purchases from used-book stores, thrift shops, and second-hand shops in general can hold the personal energy of past owners. In order to clear the old energy from any item we use a method called sageing. It involves holding fire to a sprig or bundle of dried sage until it starts to smoke, and passing the sage near the object so the smoke drifts over it. At the same time we set the intention for clearing and purifying the energy of the item. Sageing is also used to clear any area, including a person's energy field, of negative energy. We can also use a mental clearing method by focusing an intent to ground or dissipate unwanted energy.

Aside from universal energy picked up from animals, including humans, inanimate things have energy of their own. This is especially noticeable in stones. Each kind of stone has its own energy, lending that type of stone its own kind of power. While we astral traveled, Ruth and I held a polished disk of labradorite in our hands for its special properties that aid in going out-of-body. Quartz crystals have powerful characteristics. They are used for healing. They can receive, clear, hold, amplify, and transmit energy, among other things. You might recall my account of me astral flying into an asteroid that was a giant crystal geode. The energy was enormous.

Everything is connected by the universal force on all planes of existence. The same energy runs through everything, creating a glorious cosmic design of entwining patterns, each tiny part of that energy depending upon and contributing to the purpose and karma of every other part of the whole.

CONCLUSION

This book was written to give you a base of knowledge and the vocabulary to continue your investigation into metaphysics. In general, there are a vast number of subjects included under the headings of metaphysics, the occult, and new age that I have not addressed in these pages. Some subjects are included under the heading of metaphysics that do not belong there. They belong to the realms of religion, unexplained physical science such as aliens from other planets, and fantasy as in vampires. For this reason, and the fact that everyone has his own personal experience with the universal force, I did not mention everything on the subject. My intention was to present only what I know to be true from my experience, corroborated by my studies on the subject. I urge you to study further on any topic in this book that interests you, keep what makes sense to you, and seek your own truth.

GLOSSARY

<u>Akashic Record</u> – The record of everything that has happened in the past, is happening now, and will happen in the future. CHAPTER THREE

<u>animal guide</u> - Spirit guide in the form of an animal. CHAPTER EIGHT

<u>astral planes</u> – The spirit world. Places of existence that vibrate at a faster speed than in the material world. Also known as the place where disembodied souls wait to be reincarnated into the material world. CHAPTER FOUR

<u>astral travel</u> – Experiencing the planes on a higher frequency than the material plane. CHAPTER ONE

<u>aura</u> – The energy field around any living thing, including plants and stones. CHAPTER TEN

<u>chakras</u> – The energy points on our spine. CHAPTER TEN

<u>channeling</u> - Opening an energy pathway to receive messages from higher astral planes. CHAPTER SEVEN

<u>crown chakra</u> – The power point on the top of people's head that opens to the energy of the astral planes. CHAPTER TEN

<u>ectoplasm</u> – The dense energy of an earthbound departed soul. It looks like a patch of fog. CHAPTER NINE

etheric body – Life force that resides in the human body, but also exists on the astral planes. It is attached to the human body by a silver energy cord in the area of the naval. CHAPTER ONE

ghost – Earthbound energy of a person who died, sometimes seen as the grey-white fog of ectoplasm. CHAPTER NINE

immutable karma – Karma that cannot be changed, such as: a person's time of birth, parents, and place of birth. CHAPTER NINE

karma – To reap the consequences of our actions, also fate or destiny. CHAPTER SIX

kundalini – The psychic life force of the body, located in the lowest chakra on the spine. CHAPTER TEN

material plane – The densest astral plane, it vibrates at the slowest frequency. Also called the earth plane. CHAPTER FOUR

medium – A person who contacts the spirits of people who have passed away. CHAPTER NINE.

metaphysics – The study of all the astral planes, including the material plane. INTRODUCTION

oversoul (overself) – In reincarnation, an oversoul sends part of its soul down to the earth plane to live a life in order to learn lessons through its experiences. The oversoul is the repository for all the knowledge culled from all the parts of its soul's experiences in all of its material lives. CHAPTER FIVE

past life regression – Visiting the Akashic Record by astral travelling, and seeing or reenacting a past life. CHAPTER THREE

psychic rescue – Helping an earthbound soul to refocus its attention from the physical world to the spirit plane to rejoin with its oversoul. CHAPTER NINE

Reiki healing – A system of healing the physical body with the universal light through chanting and visualization. CHAPTER TEN

reincarnation – The belief that a soul after death returns to the physical plane for a new life in the body of a newborn infant. CHAPTER FIVE

silver cord - A string of energy connecting the life of a person's physical body at the navel to its etheric body (astral or energy body). CHAPTER ONE

spirit guide – An entity from the spirit world that has a message for us. CHAPTER EIGHT

third eye – The chakra (energy point) on the forehead between the eyes through which the spirit world is seen. CHAPTER TEN

totem – Specie of animal with which a person feels a soul relationship, sharing common behaviors and energies. CHAPTER TWO

trance channel – A person who opens a channel to the spirit world while he is in a hypnotic state. CHAPTER SEVEN

vortex – An open channel or doorway to the spirit world, a bridge between astral planes. CHAPTER ONE

Printed in the United States
By Bookmasters